HIGH-IMPACT TEACHING

HIGH-IMPACT TEACHING

Overcoming Student Apathy

KEEN J. BABBAGE, Ed.D.

TECHNOMIC
PUBLISHING CO., INC

LANCASTER · BASEL

High-Impact Teaching
a TECHNOMIC®publication

Published in the Western Hemisphere by
Technomic Publishing Company, Inc.
851 New Holland Avenue, Box 3535
Lancaster, Pennsylvania 17604 U.S.A.

Distributed in the Rest of the World by
Technomic Publishing AG
Missionsstrasse 44
CH-4055 Basel, Switzerland

Printed in the United States of America
10 9 8 7 6 5 4 3 2 1

Main entry under title:
    High-Impact Teaching: Overcoming Student Apathy

A Technomic Publishing Company book
Bibliography: p.
Includes index p. 171

Library of Congress Catalog Card No. 98-60210
ISBN No. 1-56676-637-0

To my mother and father

Chapter 6: Implementation Via Professional Development   133

Chapter 7: The Fascinating Adventure   149

"THE purpose of a school is to cause learning." That statement is fundamental to the ideas in my book *Meetings for School-Based Decision Making*. When a school has clearly identified its purpose, decisions are made easily if the decision that is most consistent with and most supportive of the school purpose is made.

"To every problem, there is an equal and opposite solution." That statement is fundamental to the ideas in another 1996 book of mine, *911: The School Administrator's Guide to Crisis Management*. Despite new, severe, and complex problems facing current schools, educators, and students, solutions are available; therefore, educators can confidently lead and manage schools to cause learning rather than merely accept the tyranny of unexpected events or frenzied days.

Those two fundamental concepts combine with a third premise to establish a process for making schools what they are intended to be, rather than accepting schools for what they have become.

The third premise is reached through the progression shown below:

(A) Every student can learn.

(B) Every student must learn.

(C) Every school can cause every student to learn.

(D) Every teacher can cause every one of his or her students to learn. Every teacher must cause every one of his or her students to learn.

For "D" to happen, much must occur. Students need to have adequate sleep and a good breakfast. Teachers need to be well prepared for their classes. The parents and guardians need to make sure that homework is completed. Principals need to manage funds so teachers have the necessary materials in classrooms. There are many other requirements for "D" to occur, but the emphasis in this book is classroom teaching done by classroom teachers. What can be done to expand the likelihood that every teacher will cause every student to learn? That is what this book examines: what can be done in classrooms to make school fascinating?

WHAT is preventing every teacher from causing every student to learn now? Let's create a list of possible explanations:

(1) Insufficient parental/guardian supervison

(2) Violence and vulgarity in the media

(3) Too much television

(4) Not enough emphasis on "the basics" in school

(5) Excessive governmental regulations

(6) Students passed to a higher grade before they were ready

(7) Family dysfunction

(8) Tenured teachers who are incompetent, but who are rarely fired

(9) Voters reject tax increase proposals

(10) Students who do not turn in homework

(11) Juveniles who commit crimes

(12) Parents threatening to sue school administrators or teachers

(13) Affirmative action, multiculturalism, diversity appreciation, and other social engineering

(14) Prayer was removed from public schools

(15) Children who were not read to when they were very young

(16)

(17)

(18)

(19)

(20)

(The list could continue forever, but please add your own thoughts for items 16–20.)

What answer would students give to a question about why every student is not learning in every classroom in every school? Would students mention tax initiatives that were defeated, school board policies that caused controversy, teachers getting a 2.3% pay increase instead of a 2.7% pay increase? If school exists to cause every student to learn, it is useful to ask students why they are not learning, studying, working, and behaving as far as school is concerned.

Yes, many students are making exemplary commitments to learning at school. Many teenagers and children dedicate themselves to academic success. Unfortunately, many other students make little or no effort to become educated. Also, some of the students who make good grades and who behave at school are not genuinely committed to or fascinated by school—they just do what helps avoid getting rebuked by adults.

What is one likely answer that many students would give to the question, "Why are many students not learning at school?" The chorus of children and teenagers who simultaneously respond to that question would, on the basis of what this author has heard hundreds of students say about school for two decades, say "school is boring."

How is that possible? School is the energies, imaginations, minds, and personalities of many students combined with the training, experience, minds and personalities of many educators. Would not such a collection of people create a vibrant place of countless adventures?

Teachers have various career motivations and personal motivations, but most teachers value learning, appreciate education, want to work with children or teenagers, and continue to learn throughout their careers. For most educators, learning is important, valuable, and worthwhile, and one could safely say that, although there would be a range of degree in responses from "100% agree" to "agree more than disagree," educators are people who think that "learning is fascinating."

Who is right, students or teachers? Both.

School is boring. School is a predictable, stable pattern of routine procedures. Bells ring, people move, books are opened, blanks are filled in, papers are collected, and grades are recorded. For many students, the processes at school and the experiences at school are boring and meaningless.

Learning is fascinating. Watch a child interact with a dog. The encounter is one of pure fascination as the 2-year-old learns how pets respond to people. Observe a 4-year-old jump off a diving board into the adventurous depths of a swimming pool as the instructor waits in the water. The child is excited, afraid, eager, and uncertain as he or she learns to dive.

Watch an 8-year-old at baseball practice. The tasks of fielding, running, and hitting command total concentration and complete commitment as a young athlete becomes fascinated with gaining skill in this sport.

Many children ask adults to read books to them. These children are thrilled when they start recognizing words and remembering the story. They are learning, and they are fascinated.

A 12-year-old comes to middle school and is lost in a new place amid 800 people. This student is determined to find her way around the building. She sees some friends from elementary school. She is sure that a boy smiled at her. Middle school band class begins with the theme music from the most popular movie of the summer. Middle school is going to be fascinating, she thinks. By the end of the first week and by the completion of twelve typical worksheets, the only fascination left is that the boy who smiled at her has said he may call her this weekend.

A 16-year-old preparing for the tests that lead to earning a driver's license is an example of a teenager whose learning process cannot be denied. He studies the manual so he can pass the written test and earn a temporary driver's permit. He is absolutely obsessed with driving a car. He may also become interested in the mechanics of the car. He will encounter realities such as the cost of car insurance, the cost of a traffic ticket, or the cost of gas. He is fascinated with the possibilities provided by earning a driver's license.

The best teacher in the best class this author has attended was purely fascinating. Students got to that class early to claim front-row seats. That teacher was not working at the best school I have attended. That teacher was far better than most of his colleagues. He created an island of fascination in an ocean of the ordinary. What he did in the classroom could have been matched or surpassed by other teachers. What kept them from being fascinating teachers? What kept their classrooms from being fascinating places?

School is boring, but some parts of school are fascinating. Notice how hard students work at marching band practices, sports practices, rehearsal for a play, or a school newspaper editing session. What fascinates students about these activities? Notice how captivated many students are in some classrooms? What is occurring in those classrooms that inspires such awe?

Some cynics have lamented that we waste education on the young. The reasoning must be that 13-year-olds do not appreciate education. I disagree. We waste the inherent curiosity, energy, and spirit of adventure in young people on the boring processes that too often make up a typical day at school.

Time out. I know the complaint. "Students are supposed to do what they are told at school. We can't just spend each day at school letting them have fun, goof off, and waste time. There is work to do."

Students do have responsibilities. Students are required to be at school daily, on time, prepared for class, with homework completed, and with behavior under control. Teachers also have responsibilities, one of which is to cause every student to learn. One way to help each student to learn is to make each class a fascinating adventure as students, the teacher, knowledge, and experiences interact in ways that cause learning.

There are many wonderful teachers whose classrooms are already fascinating places. Thank you for showing students and colleagues how fascinating school can be. The ideas in this book may help you do an even better job or may help you identify ways to share your expertise with your colleagues.

For the many eager college students or graduate students preparing to become teachers, this book can help you prepare for the career you await.

There are many school administrators who are seeking ways to inspire discouraged teachers, to invigorate exhausted teachers, or to improve average and below average teachers. The ideas in this book could help those administrators work with those teachers to create schools where learning is caused in every classroom for, with, and by every student.

There are many ordinary school administrators and teachers whose schools and classrooms are brain-dead dungeons where the textbook, worksheets and occasional video cassettes are the most common methods used. The ideas in this book are offered as a less intrusive procedure, but are intended to be as dramatic as a brain transplant.

There are many conscientious students who make an admirable commitment to school and who are personally fascinated with learning. Keep it up. There are many other students who see school as a total waste of time. They have some legitimate complaints, but they also need to quit making excuses and start accepting responsibilities. To the conscientious and apathetic students, we owe the most fascinating education possible.

Students are fascinating people. Getting to know them is such a compelling adventure that it makes me one of the educators who does not prefer the days, weeks, and months when school is closed. Interacting with students in the classroom is a priceless, precious duty and joy. Other interactions at school, even for discipline purposes, can cause learning and can build some mutual trust.

Teaching is hard work. My colleagues who are retiring from teaching or from school administration tell me how much more difficult their work has been recently than when their careers began. They often say, "We're just dealing with a different type of student." I translate their statement into these conclusions: (1) a higher percentage of students in school are misbehaving, but it is still a small percentage; (2) the misbehaviors in schools now are worse than in earlier years; and (3) some students make little or no effort to learn, but most students are still people with who we can work and who we can educate in a standard school. I also ask this question: because we are dealing with a different type of student, isn't it sensible to consider different ways of teaching these students?

This book is built upon two ideas: (1) for many students, school is boring; however, (2) for any person, the experience of learning—when and where it does happen—is fascinating. The purpose of a school is to cause learning. To any problem that gets in the way of learning, there is a solution; therefore, schools should be places where learning is caused and the participants in that learning experience the total, constant fascination that is inherent in real learning.

The blame for boredom in schools can be shared among many people. This book will emphasize the work that can be done in the classrooms to make school fascinating. Most of what students experience in school happens in classrooms and most of what happens in classrooms can be determined by teachers.

My experience as a teacher and as a school administrator is in grades 6–12; therefore, the perspective of this book is directed to secondary schools. It is hoped that teachers in other levels can apply some ideas in this book with appropriate adjustments. Some trends in education or among students do start with high school and move down the age range, so current boredom toward schools by many secondary school students may be for reasons that are or soon will be shared by elementary school students.

I have worked outside of education in great jobs with three large corporations. The experience obtained in those jobs taught me to look beyond the ordinary sources of solutions. To the extent that ideas in this book seem to be atypical, that is by design. Solutions to the problems of education can be found in many places if we permit ourselves to look and to think "outside of the box" of traditional solutions. We cannot solve today's problem of students who dismiss school as boring, meaningless, and irrelevant using only yesterday's, yesteryear's, and yesterdecade's ideas from education sources only.

Also, as a college student, I took a theater class, and I acted in one play. I had never done anything associated with theater, drama, or acting before. When I became a teacher, I applied those skills and concepts from acting daily. Again, educators may find ideas and solutions from unexpected sources.

In the summer of 1996, I attended several baseball games to watch my then 8-year-old nephew play. He is a very capable young athlete, and he is a superior student at school. In one baseball game, he had a particularly difficult time at bat. Twice he swung and missed. Twice more, he swung and barely tipped the baseball into foul territory. What would happen with the next pitch? Whack. He smashed a hit to right field. After the game I asked him, "What were you thinking that time you had two strikes?"

He quickly replied, "I just kept believing that I would get a hit." My nephew's belief was accompanied by total concentration, commitment, and effort. He was fascinated with the challenge of hitting the baseball. Belief, proper work, and fascination produced the desired result.

I keep believing that we will make every classroom and every school places where every student is fascinated with learning and is taught by fascinating teachers. That belief combined with proper work can produce the desired fascinating result: to cause learning by every student in every classroom.

During his 1968 presidential campaign, Robert Kennedy often said, "Some people see things as they are and ask 'why?'; I dream things that never were and ask 'why not?' "

Applying that perspective to education, "Some educators see schools as they are and say 'Could be worse. We're good enough'; I see schools and say 'Could be better. What can we do to improve?' " This book offers ideas and ways to improve schools via teaching that fascinates students and teachers.

Again using the structure and reasoning that Robert Kennedy provided, "Some people see problems in education and ask for more money. I see problems in education and ask for more commitment, productivity, and ideas."

For every person who chose teaching as a career and/or who was chosen by teaching to enter this vital profession, there is a hope that each student can become an academic superstar. Years of teaching can exhaust, frustrate, and discourage the most capable and the most determined teacher. This book says to that veteran teacher, here's a way to ignite anew your original conviction and to ignite a renaissance in the minds of your students.

For every teacher who has said, "How can I reach these students?" this book offers a plan that you can implement immediately. No new money is required, and no new laws have to be passed. You can take charge right now in your classroom.

For every administrator who has wondered, "What can I do to help that teacher do the work I know he or she is capable of doing?" this book says, show that teacher the teaching process that seeks to fascinate and that by fascinating can also help with classroom management, staff morale, and school climate.

This book says that teachers and administrators today are being asked to do superhuman work against unprecedented difficulties, so a way to get the desired results without increasing budgets or increasing workloads is needed. Although many solutions could be imposed on schools, this book contends that the most effective solutions will be implemented in classrooms and will impact the priceless exchange between teachers and students.

As I walked to the bus loading area today after school dismissal to supervise students as they left school, an 8th grader smiled at me as I walked behind him and his friends. They were walking home. Showing the pure imagination and energetic creativity of a student, he said to me. "Hey, you can't come spend the night until my mom says it's OK."

I paused and realized that his was a spontaneous moment of impromptu theater. I replied, "Well, my mom said it was OK." We laughed long and loudly.

Such an exchange is one reminder of how clever, bright, imaginative, and unpredictable students can be. If we tap their curiosity and their eagerness to be fascinated, we can teach them all we have dreamed of teaching, plus we can learn with them. Let the fascination begin, and may the boredom fade away.

KEEN BABBAGE

CHAPTER 1

The Continuing Debate and Some Unexpected Common Ground

From the 1890s through the 1990s, one of the several constants in American public education has been a continuing debate about "What is wrong with our public schools?" The curriculum has been revised for each generation, the grade levels assigned to junior highs or middle schools have changed, the design of school buildings tried to keep up with new educational philosophies, and endless new programs were created to deal with each new task assigned to schools.

The debate continues today. Should we adopt a national curriculum? Should we have students demonstrate mastery of certain skills and knowledge prior to moving to the next grade? Can we establish a clear set of academic standards for all students? Should we abolish the Department of Education in Washington, D.C., and decentralize all education back to the states and the communities? Should students wear school uniforms? How do we remove drugs, weapons, and violence from schools?

The debate has to be heard and understood, but the debaters need to listen and think as much as they talk and criticize. There could be some unexpected common ground. The goal of this chapter is to reveal the unexpected.

"THE Chamber of Commerce will sponsor a community forum about our public school system. Everyone is invited to participate in this event, which will be held next Tuesday night at 7:00 P.M. in the auditorium of Johnson High School. Parents, guardians, students, teachers, citizens, business leaders, media members, and everyone else who has ideas or concerns about our schools should come and voice their thoughts. The meeting will be broadcast over local cable television. Your thoughts can be faxed in or mailed in if you cannot attend. Send those to the Chamber of Commerce. All input will be compiled and put into the form of recommendations that will be made to the school board. Call the Chamber of Commerce office for more information."

That script was read over the local radio stations and television stations in Johnson City, a typical American community of about 180,000 people. The

1

city has a varied economy with several new manufacturing plants plus lots of farmland nearby. There is a state regional university, and there are two private colleges in the community. The community has one public school district that resulted when the old county system and two smaller public districts within the county boundaries merged about 20 years ago.

In recent years, there have been many successes in the school district. National merit scholars have graduated from the three local high schools and have attended Ivy League universities. One high school has won three state football championships. Several teachers have been state finalists for teacher of the year. One principal was honored nationally for her work with children from low-income homes. Several school/parent groups have begun tutoring programs that were featured on a national television program for helping reduce the drop-out rate.

Still, the citizens of Johnson City have become increasingly concerned about their public school system in recent years. There are two new private schools that have opened, and they seem to be attracting more students each year. The local daily newspaper and the local weekly newspaper report that more teachers are retiring early or quitting altogether, plus there are reports of violence at some school almost weekly. Business people, especially those at the new manufacturing plants, report that it is difficult to find enough capable employees locally.

The Chamber of Commerce members asked themselves what could be done about these growing concerns. Their solution was to host a public forum about education. They knew that it would be a risk to let people come and express their frustrations, fears, worries, and criticisms, but they concluded that progress had to begin with some effort to understand what the current reality was or at least what people perceived to be reality in and about schools.

The president of the Chamber of Commerce opened the forum with these comments: "Thank you for being here tonight. My name is Paula Franklin, and I am the president of the Chamber of Commerce. We all know that our students deserve the best possible education. If you have lived here for a long time, you know that our schools were once the best in the state, maybe the best in many states. We still have a good school system, but many things have changed, and many people in Johnson City have become concerned about our public schools.

"The Chamber of Commerce thinks that improvement of our schools begins with a complete discussion of the concerns and ideas that people have about those schools, so that is why we are here tonight. I'll call each person to the microphone in the order that you signed up. We will stay until the last person who would like to speak has been heard. Try to keep your comments to 3 minutes, please. If you have written your comments, you may leave a copy with me. Our first speaker is Thomas Morrison."

Mr. Morrison: I'm a retired teacher. I taught for 8 years in Cincinnati and then for 22 years in Johnson City. I retired in 1994, and I do some substitute teaching now. Here's my concern. This school district keeps worrying about statistics that show 8th grade girls do better in school than boys do or 4th grade reading levels are higher with one gender or ethnic group than another. The drop-out rate is higher with low-income students than with middle-income students. So, the district hires extra people to go work with the group that is not succeeding. Wait a minute. This school district is giving every student an opportunity to be educated. Is each family making sure that their child is at school on time, behaves, completes homework, and comes to school with proper respect for teachers?

I never hear the school board get upset when one demographic group is over-represented in basketball or in free and reduced lunch, but if boys do better with math in high school than girls do, the high school math teachers are the first suspects. From my experience, this school district gives equal opportunity to all students. The district should not be expected to require equal results for every student. I hate to see students fail, but I hate even more to see adults make excuses for those students. The issue is not equal opportunity. The issue is responsibility. Until every family and every student accepts responsibility for the educational success of each child, no new programs will matter.

One other thing. It's tougher to teach now than it used to be. People argue too much now. I call a parent to explain how their son or daughter spoke to me in class, and the adult on the phone speaks in a more ugly way. Plus, so many students now just don't care about school and education. They come to school only to eat lunch and act silly. It's not fair to everyone else.

Ms. Franklin: Thank you, Mr. Morrison. We'll take a moment now for our other speakers to get lined up. Please sit in the front rows according to the number you were given when you signed the list of speakers. When the speaker ahead of you finishes, or when I tell them that time is up, please move to the microphone.

Ms. Harvey: I'm a grandmother. I have two granddaughters who are in our school system. They live with me, and I'm their guardian. I know that it must be harder to teach these days because it is a lot harder to bring up children today. These teenagers have such a defiant attitude and such vulgar language. They hate school. Getting them to do homework is impossible. I need someone to tell me how I get them to like school. I loved school. My sons and my daughter liked school. These grandchildren keep telling me how dull school is. I tell them that school is not entertainment. I tell them that school work is interesting, but they just tell me about dull teachers and textbooks that are dull. What do I do to get these children excited about school?

Ms. Rooney: I appreciate the opportunity to be heard tonight. I've been thinking a lot about schools since I watched C-SPAN a year or so back when they covered that education summit conference that governors and corporate leaders had. Everyone there talked about standards. The idea, I guess, was that if we tell every student and teacher that they have to do better, well, they will suddenly start doing better or they will at least try to reach the new standard. Something is missing from that idea. Are governors going to pass laws that require students to study more or that require teachers to teach better? It's just not as simple as that summit tried to make it.

I own an advertising business. We have clients from this state and others. Our job is to help clients succeed in the marketplace. We design advertising, marketing, and promotions. We help businesses determine what consumers want and need, then we help those businesses present their products or services. Do schools ever advertise? Do schools promote learning as their product the way businesses promote soft drinks or clothes? I mean, children and teenagers get excited about soft drinks and clothes for lots of reasons, including all of the advertising and marketing that make those products seem exciting.

Our employees are responsible for bringing in new business while also doing great work for our current clients. Is there any way to get educators to think like that? Our employees are not guaranteed a job because clients can leave us and go to another advertising agency. Educators seem to think that they deserve their job whether they get results or not.

So, my real concern is that we deal with any education problem right where the best solution is. It seems to me that education happens in classrooms, not in governors' offices or corporate headquarters. My request is that we emphasize changes in classrooms as we consider solutions.

Mr. Welch: Let's get serious. The taxpayers in Johnson City pay enough taxes to have the world's best schools: local taxes, state taxes, property taxes, sales taxes, cable television taxes, and others that we don't even know about. Enough. Where does all the money go? I read the papers and the national news publications. I know that we spend more on education now than ever. What are we getting for our money? I'll tell you. We're getting high-school graduates who cannot read, 13-year-olds running wild at night, and schools with paid babysitters for their students who have had babies. Don't ask me to pay one penny more until you can show me that every employee of the schools is busting their rear end to get every student to learn.

I saw that newspaper story about a shortage of substitute teachers. Well, let those high-paid administrators in the big offices go substitute teach once a week. They'll get a taste of reality then. It would be their most demanding work in some time I expect, plus it might remind them that the best way to help schools is to improve what happens in classrooms.

One other thing. What's wrong with our newspaper? My son makes straight A grades. He has never been in trouble at school. He is a high school junior. He's in National Honor Society, Beta Club, Chess Club, Marching Band, and Academic Team. His Academic Team was third in the state recently. Third in the state! The newspaper had a tiny story about that, and they stuck it on some obscure page. Now, it is almost basketball season, and the newspaper runs a huge special section about high-school basketball and about junior high-school basketball. What are students supposed to make of all that? Simple, putting a ball through a hoop is more important than putting a correct answer to a question. I love sports. I played high-school basketball. I coach a soccer team now. Let's just give equal time to academics.

Mr. Korman: I teach at the local university. My children attend private schools. I'm a taxpayer. I'm asking that our community study the voucher system that Milwaukee has used. Why can't we give more choices to families? If I pay taxes for schools, am I not entitled to a portion of the total tax money so I can send my children where I think they should go to school. If I choose public schools, the money goes to public schools. If I prefer a private school, that same money goes with my children to the private school. If the public schools do not have the expense of educating my children why should the public schools get the money to educate my children?

If you have the best teachers and the best teaching, my children will come to the public schools. I'd pay extra for that quality.

Ms. Lefield: I would like to ask that we study the idea of students wearing a uniform at school. Schools just aren't safe anymore. Some students bring drugs or weapons. Students threaten each other, steal, and fight. Teachers feel unsafe. A school uniform can help remove some of the reasons for the unrest at school. If students wear $500 worth of designer clothes, they create a distraction or maybe even a temptation for a fight. Students and teachers, too, should dress to work and to learn, not to play or be casual.

Tell me this, why do so many teachers dress like it is a day off? Jeans and a golf shirt just don't impress me. Teachers want to be seen as professionals, so they need to look that way. They get full-time pay, and they get summers off. Come on, at least look like you are a professional adult worker when you are trying to get students to take you seriously. I agree—what matters most is what happens in the classrooms and the example set by the teacher in everything, including appearance, probably matters more than any law or any idea from that high-level education summit.

Mr. Burkell: I'm a teacher. I love to teach. I care about students— I've devoted myself for 21 years to students. Let's think about the past 21 years. We got rid of the new math, schools without walls, and several other unsuccessful fads. We moved from the days of when a student misbehaves at school he or she gets punished at home to when a student misbehaves at school the parent or guardian blames us, goes to our superiors, and threatens a lawsuit. We've seen affirmative action in hiring and multicultural additions to the curriculum. Christmas vacation is now winter break. We have more 4-day weeks than any other profession, and that means losing more momentum than our longer vacations in December, April, and the summer already cost us. We've seen the epidemic of Attention Deficit Disorder create a debate over whether that condition is a real malady or an expensive excuse. We see the curriculum being asked to include Aids awareness, African-American history, women in history, conflict resolution, emphasis on basic academic skills plus emphasis on higher order thinking, inclusion of Special Education students in more mainstream classes, and an increased need for alternative schools for disruptive, defiant, and violent students. We have metal detectors, weapons, drugs, and violence in some schools.

Now, take all of that, and to the credit of everyone who has not quit or taken early retirement, we still educate students. How can we best educate all students is my question, because getting a good enough education for most students is not good enough? How can we best educate all students?

Well, let's be honest. Schools today are not what they were a generation ago. Still, most students behave, and most students do their work. The percentage of disruptive students is up. Their misbehavior is worse, more disruptive, and more serious than in earlier years. We need to create new educational institutions for the students who cannot or will not function in standard schools. Alternative schools, boot camps, residential facilities, and others are needed. Also, stealing at school is stealing, but it rarely results in court action as it could if it happened elsewhere. Some close partnership between schools and the juvenile justice system could help.

The common solutions, such as higher standards, national curriculum, vouchers, charter schools, abolish the department of education, or revise teacher tenure laws are simplistic. I'm a teacher. I know how to teach. My students learn. I'd suggest that our profession admit that some teaching methods work and other teaching methods fail. Let's require the teachers not to do what they have always done or to do what is available, but to do what works. Principals need to be supported when they require teachers to use effective methods just like a factory manager must be supported when requiring that employees do what works, not what they like.

Ms. Hamler: I liked those magnet schools we used to have. Most of them have changed back to regular schools. I think people lost interest in them, but I hope we can review the idea of magnet schools or, at least, that schools could use some good ideas that the magnet schools used.

My children tell me that what they dislike about school is the routine. Their teachers open a textbook in August and just plod through the book and the worksheets that come with the book. Occasionally, they have a teacher who brings in lots of different materials and includes a variety of activities while still using the textbook as a foundation. My children love the classes with all that variety. It just doesn't happen very often, so the children tell me how dull school is. I always liked school. I wish they did.

Paul Cavendish: I'm a high-school senior. I've been assigned to attend this forum as a project for my political science class. I thought I would hear people talking about students, since that is what schools are for. Instead, I hear all kinds of comments about vouchers or taxes.

So, here's my idea. A student who wears a uniform can be violent. A student whose family had choices of what school to select can be disruptive. A student at a magnet school can skip class. Students who reject today's standards can reject new standards. Students who do not care about the local curriculum aren't going to care about a national curriculum.

School is boring. It's that simple. School is boring. The textbooks are dull. The assignments are dull. The tests are predictable. The hand-outs that teachers copy from some book are no better than homework I copy from a student—nobody learns from that. It's not uniforms or all the other ideas that matter. It's whether school is interesting or not. Bored students in baggy pants would be bored students in school uniforms unless school became interesting.

Mr. Brown: I graduated from college 36 years ago. I still learn all I can whenever I can. Learning is fascinating. I'm sorry to hear that school is boring to some students.

I do wish that we could find ways to make the summer more productive for students. They go to school about 180 days. That is only half of a calendar year. Summer is often wasted by many children and teenagers. The school buildings are available in the summer. Can't we create some ways to bring students to school for new experiences in the summer?

Ms. Hunter: Are we doing enough in our schools with technology? Computer literacy is essential for students who will work in the twenty-first century. Computers can do a lot of instruction, including individual instruction. Today's software takes the place of a library. Students can visit any part of the world with computers, and they can access any data. Self-instruction is efficient. If we had enough computers in schools, each student could move at his or her own pace. Lots of school records and secretarial duties could be handled on computer. I just want to be sure that our schools do not get left behind in the information revolution.

Ms. Jandor: My children attend private schools because the public schools have taken religion out of education. Also, the private schools my children attend have after-school programs each afternoon until 5:30. My family counts on that supervision. If the public schools could just have opportunities for students to gather and pray, we would be pleased. If some after school supervision could be included, we would be very supportive. I know that the public schools can't do what each special group requests, but I wanted to offer those ideas.

Ms. Franklin: We've heard from everyone who signed up to speak prior to the start of the meeting. Three more people have asked to speak since the meeting began. That is fine.

Ms. Mellen: I work with the state association of student councils. Each summer, we train several hundred middle-school and high-school students in leadership skills. They attend a workshop for a week. They really get interested in the workshop. They never get bored. They fascinate themselves with how much can be learned and with the different ways to learn. Some of our methods could be used in classrooms.

Also, I teach middle school, and I coach soccer. The soccer players work hard at each practice and in each game. I teach the way I coach. The students in the classroom work as hard as the students on the soccer team. It can be done. Taxes do not have to go up to get better results in schools. Sure, we need enough money, but more money alone never guarantees better results. The quality of our work, the productivity of our work, and the proven methods we use are important.

Christy Matthews: I'm in the same political science class that Paul is in. There is one thought I'd like to add, please. When I talk to my friends who go to other schools, they tell me what is good or bad at their school. I tell them the same about mine. We usually talk about teachers, the ones who are tough and those who are easy, the ones we take seriously and the ones who are just taking up space. It seems to me that every school has some good things and some good teachers. Can't we just take all the good ideas from all schools and share them with everyone? Wouldn't that be easy and inexpensive? Maybe the best ideas would make school less boring, maybe even make school interesting so students would want to learn.

Ms. Kristen: I'm a parent of three students in our schools. My three children are very different. One is a scholar. He's in the gifted program at a middle school. One is a hard worker, but needs lots of help in reading because of a learning disability. Her school does great work in special education for her. Now, the oldest has a C-plus average and always has. There's nothing for him. He's between gifted and special education. I hear that all students can learn and can succeed. I know that my oldest gets tired of being stuck in the middle. What can be done to move him up to better grades? Do we know how to help C students become B students?

Ms. Franklin: I want to thank everyone for their comments and ideas. The Chamber of Commerce will include your thoughts in our report and in our recommendations to the school board.

CHAMBER OF COMMERCE REPORT

We conclude that quality education is vital to continuing the quality of life our community expects. We further conclude that quality education is within reach, but is not yet within our grasp.

The bottom line in education is how much and how well students learn. Many factors impact that bottom line, but within the control of the local school district, no factor is more potent than the effectiveness of classroom teachers. We place our emphasis on that factor.

This school district has many superior teachers whose students are captivated, who are fascinated, who are successful, and who are learning. What are those teachers doing?

This school district also has some average or below average teachers whose students are bored, are passing time, and who are not learning much. What are those teachers not doing? We believe that those teachers want to be effective and want their students to succeed in school. We are asking that those teachers be shown methods, processes, and ideas that can help them do the quality work we believe they are capable of and eager to do so their students can learn.

We conclude that before any major or minor changes are made in our school district—vouchers, magnet schools, year-round schedules, alternative schools, new standards, or curriculum changes—an intense study be conducted in the district's classrooms to identify the very specific and very imitable actions, ideas, methods, and practices that effective teachers are using. Each principal knows who are the effective teachers at each school—those teachers and principals who observe their work will be key sources of input. Also, community members will be surveyed to obtain additional ideas about effective teachers. It is hoped that these community members can share the methods that their teachers used to inspire learning. This input will then be put into a handbook and a training program for all of the district's teachers to experience, including the good teachers because they will want to become better, we trust.

Until the school district is convinced that each teacher in each classroom is doing what is necessary to teach, to fascinate, and to create commitment from each student, the need for other possible actions cannot be evaluated accurately. We do advise the district to obtain information about education reform, but to delay any structural, organizational, or policy changes until the classroom teaching changes we envision are implemented.

If every problem in every school needs a new program to solve that problem, schools will be overwhelmed with well-intentioned programs and with the bureaucracies that programs create.

If one solution could solve all problems in schools, that one solution would be applauded, approved, and implemented immediately. Education is more complex and more complicated than the power of any one solution; however, some solutions are more comprehensive in impact than others.

Creating teaching that fascinates students so that they learn and become committed to learning is suggested in this book as one such comprehensive solution to current educational problems. Students who find school fascinating could also find school worth attending, worth behaving at, and worth completing; therefore, truancy, discipline, and drop-out problems could be impacted.

Teachers want students to learn, to succeed in school, and to be prepared for a lifetime of challenges and opportunities. Many current teachers find their work frustrating and exhausting. Some teachers find their workplaces to be frightening and dangerous. Parents who never visit school, but who blame teachers for their child failing can cause the best teacher to be stressed. Students who refuse to do homework, who disrupt class, and who start fights can make any teacher reconsider his or her career choice. Students who are apathetic about school, who never try, who let their brain atrophy, and who waste their ability cause anguish in the heart, mind, and soul of any teacher who intended to make a difference in the life of each student.

Students want school to interest them, to not bore them, to be worth their effort, and to never be dull. Students seek applications of their energy, curiosity, imagination, restlessness, and wonder. If learning can do that for students, they will learn. Learning may not be their goal. Doing something "neat," "cool," or "fun" may be their goal, but if learning comes along with interesting experiences that apply their youthful energy and curiosity, everyone benefits.

Taxpayers expect the school system to have safe, productive places that graduate literate, competent, civil young adults. Employers expect schools to prepare trained and trainable workers. Conservatives expect school to teach a proper respect for our nation's traditional curriculum and traditional ethics. Liberals expect school to teach students to inquire, analyze, question, and learn how to learn. The list of groups that make demands on schools is endless, and trying to completely satisfy each of those groups is futile; however, there could be enough common ground to declare a time-out in the existing education battle and put the energy of the combatants into a common effort.

Teachers want students to learn. Students want school to not bore them. Parents and guardians, taxpayers and employers, conservatives and liberals, interest groups and the media expect schools to be productive in the work of educating students. Could there be some common ground? Yes.

Teachers want students to learn. Will students learn when the process of learning fascinates them? It seems reasonable to say yes.

Students want school to not be boring. If school provided constantly fascinating experiences, could students find school worth their best effort? Again, yes is a reasonable answer and expectation.

If classrooms become places of productive, fulfilling, intellectual, commitment building, fascinating experiences that cause learning that teachers and students find meaningful, the results that other groups seek could be reached.

The critics will shout, "That's too easy, too simplistic. It will never work." Establish a school in which every class period is a fascinating experience for teachers and students before any final conclusion is drawn. Is there such a school? Maybe not. Is such a school possible? Yes! Are there magnet schools, high-technology schools, voucher plans, schools with students wearing uniforms, and schools with metal detectors? Yes. Are all of those schools reaching every educational goal? Unlikely.

I have seen fascinated students. They work. They learn. They behave. They get along with each other. They do not skip school.

I have seen bored students. Some work, others do nothing. Some learn, others pass time. Some behave, others disrupt. Some get along, others get violent. Some attend, others are truant.

Let's ask students to complete this question:

The school I attend is _____ boring   _____ fascinating.

Let's ask teachers to answer this question:

Learning is _____ boring   _____ fascinating.

It is reasonable that many students would respond that school is boring. It is reasonable that many or most (all?) teachers would respond that learning is fascinating. We have discovered the unexpected common ground—when school is fascinating to students, students will be fascinated with learning at school.

Will fascinating teaching and learning work for every student? No, some students will still be defiant, violent, and incorrigible. They probably need to be taught elsewhere. Will this work for most students? Isn't it worth finding out? Creating fascination in classrooms is a no cost, no tax increase, no new laws method of reducing teachers' frustration, increasing teachers' productivity, and increasing teachers' job satisfaction while also reducing student failure, increasing student success, and increasing student learning.

Fascination in the classroom may not solve every educational problem, but boredom is related to many serious educational problems. Eliminating or reducing boredom can have multiple benefits. Robert Bork, in his best selling book *Slouching Toward Gomorrah,* concluded that "Boredom is a much underrated emotion. The young, especially the very intelligent and vigorous, who have not yet found a path in life are particularly susceptible to boredom's relentless ache. It is an emotion that is dangerous for individuals and for society because a lot of the cures are anti-social: alcohol, narcotics, cruelty, pornography, violence, zealotry in a political cause" (p. 23). Could some similar misbehaviors emerge from students who are bored?

Fascinating classrooms are not a panacea. There is no panacea. Fascinating classrooms are a sensible, logical, and feasible educational idea that could do much good while having little or no potential for doing harm. Why has this idea not been thought of or tried before? Because causing learning via creating constant fascination in classrooms is not required by schools, but is known to be effective by great teachers who love their work because they are fascinated with students and students are fascinated with learning in their classes.

In the next chapter, the symbiotic realities of teacher, student, parent, guardian, and community will be further explored with an eye toward implementing fascinating classrooms, creating fascinating schools, and making school as fascinating as learning is.

CHAPTER 2

We Are in This Together

Schools must be safe, orderly places. Schools do not have to be somber, comatose places. Classrooms, especially, should be vibrant, vivid, energetic, creative, fascinating places.

All too often, school is boring. In an attempt to "cover material" or "keep every student on task," teachers can get in the habit of relying on classroom activities that lull and that dull students into submissive compliance.

With an excuse of "there just isn't enough time," teachers may often rely on textbooks, worksheets, last year's or last decade's lesson plans, textbook publisher-provided tests, and questions at the end of a chapter to fill the days in a school year.

Lost in these pedantic routines is the spirit of fascination that could fill each classroom as teachers and students intensely interact with ideas, with experiences, with thoughts, with questions, with facts, with concepts, with responsibilities, and with each other.

Students often say that "School is boring." Teachers increasingly comment that "Students just don't care about school. They just aren't interested. They should want to learn."

Those two comments are mirror images of one another. Students would prefer that school be fascinating. Teachers would prefer that students display a genuine fascination with and energetic involvement in learning. Students and teachers may share a common goal without realizing it—classrooms that are vibrant places with fascinated people interacting with fascinating ideas and activities that cause learning.

Students are fascinating. Learning is fascinating. Why are schools so often filled with classrooms that are boring? What does happen in classrooms where students are fascinated with learning? To begin exploring these topics, we first look at school through the perspective of students.

SCHOOL—A STUDENT'S PERSPECTIVE

"WHERE are my Nike shoes? Who took my Nikes?" Jared's question was directed to everyone in his family who was still at home. "Come on, the school bus will be here in a minute. I need those shoes."

Jared's parents had already left for work on this Monday morning. Jared's older brother would leave soon and drive to his high school. His sister, Ellen, a perfect student who never got in trouble, was walking out the front door to be early for the bus that would take Jared and her to middle school.

Jared found the shoes right where he left them the day before. "I'm gone, Andy," he yelled at his brother. Jared got to the bus stop as the bus arrived. Of course, Jared and his sister sat far apart on the bus. Jared joined his friends who were in an energetic conversation.

"Yeah, well nobody beats the Bulls. They rule. Who can beat the Chicago Bulls?"

"They are the best."

"Well, how about us. Who is trying out for the school team?"

"Who cares about the school team. When school is out, I leave that place. I'm not staying for no basketball practice."

"You're crazy. Basketball is the best thing about school. People come and cheer for you. The girls are impressed."

"What girl is impressed with you?" Your sister?"

"At least my sister and I know who our parents are."

"Back off you guys. Back off. It ain't worth a fight."

"Hey, did anybody see that TV show last night about same-sex marriages. It was different."

"I saw some of it, but then my mother turned it off! She said it was too strange for her. I just figure everyone decides for themselves."

"I watched that other movie about nuclear war. He got $10 million to be in that movie. That's me someday."

"Yeah, right. How you going to be in the movies? You can't even pass 8th grade. How you going anywhere?"

As the bus arrived at school, the sorting process was apparent. Smart students who make good grades and stay out of trouble went straight to class, making sure they had all homework ready to turn in. Future drop-outs headed for a bathroom to create a plan for skipping school but catching the school bus home so their family never knew. Athletes were hanging out by the gym. New students looked lost and probably were lost. The great majority of students associated with their friends in groups of two to ten—middle school students often travel in groups—and generally started moving toward class. The warning bell at 7:59 A.M. got some reaction from most people still in the hallways. By 8:00 A.M., almost everyone was in class.

A Very Boring Class

Jared had science class from 8:00–8:55 A.M. Everything Jared and his friends talked about on the bus could relate to science: shooting a basketball, improving athletic performance, how television shows are transmitted, and how different societies structure families. Jared might be surprised by how useful science is. Unfortunately, today would be one more boring day in Ms. Armstrong's science class. Maybe Ms. Armstrong would be surprised with how useful science is and how fascinating science class can be.

About 10 minutes into class, Jared asked Ms. Armstrong a question. "What's the point of this, Ms. Armstrong? I just can't get the point of it." Jared was genuinely and politely wondering what the point of the assignment was.

The teacher paused. Her first thought was to accuse the student of being disrespectful, but Ms. Armstrong realized that Jared's question was sincere. Her second thought was unclear, but she managed to reply: "It's, uh, it's very close to some work you'll do in high school."

Jared was polite and did not challenge the unconvincing answer. He wished that the principal would call Ms. Armstrong to the office and send another teacher. Jared knew that he would make a good grade in science, but he also knew that every minute in science would be painfully boring.

On this day, Ms. Armstrong's students were completing a worksheet about the solar system. Yesterday, they completed a worksheet about the solar system. Tomorrow, they would begin reading a chapter in their textbook about the solar system. As they would read the chapter silently and individually, they would also write answers to questions at the end of each section in the chapter. In a few days, they would have a test—probably a machine-graded, textbook publisher-provided, multiple-choice test like all of Ms. Armstrong's other tests—on the solar system.

Jared had heard other students make rude comments about Ms. Armstrong. He also heard teachers talk about her. One teacher said, "Her paycheck should be sent to the textbook publisher—they do all her work." Another teacher said, "She's no teacher, she's a classroom clerk." Jared had enough reasons to stay out of trouble, so he avoided any gossip about teachers, but he really wished he could learn more about the solar system. Space seemed so neat to Jared when he saw a news report of a rocket launched or when the last eclipse happened.

"Finally," Jared said softly when the bell rang to end science class. The students erupted with conversation. Fifty-five minutes of worksheets can result in much pent-up conversation and energy.

"Did you finish that science, Kim?" Jared asked his friend.

"Are you kidding? Most of us never do the science. We still get a passing grade. Hey, did you hear about Josh and Jason? They're busted."

"What happened?" Jared asked as they walked from their lockers to social studies class.

"Josh and Jason left their houses about midnight Saturday. They got caught about 2:00 in the morning by a policeman over by the mall. They were driving somebody's car, but they are too young to drive. That's why they aren't here today."

A Very Fascinating Class

Jared and Kim took their seats in Mr. Prather's social studies class. They would continue their conversation after class or at lunch.

Today's social studies lesson dealt with the process a local city council uses to consider a new law or ordinance. The topic being considered was a day-time curfew. The community already had a night curfew for teenagers. The proposed idea would apply to the hours when school is in session. Any person of school age who was not at school and who was seen on the streets or anywhere else without a parent or guardian would be subject to questioning, citation, or arrest by a police officer or school security officer.

The students took the roles of mayor, city council members, news reporters, citizens, police officers, and city employees. They did more than read about, hear about, or do worksheets about a city council meeting—they convincingly and realistically conducted a city council meeting. Their guest was a former city council member who participated by playing the role of an angry citizen and who evaluated the students' meeting in a very lively, inter-active discussion with the students.

Jared's favorite part of the class was when the student who acted as the city's attorney was asked if the proposed law would violate the first amendment protection for freedom of assembly. The answer given was "Freedoms have limits. The freedom to drive is taken away if you keep breaking the speed limit. The freedom to speak is limited if you intentionally lie about people. The freedom to assemble cannot mean any people, any place, any time, for any reason."

At that point, Kim leaned over to Jared and said, "Does that mean we don't have to assemble in that boring science class tomorrow?"

Mr. Prather concluded class just before the bell. "Great job today. I'm impressed with your work. Tomorrow, our city council will vote on the proposed law in class so lobby the students who are council members today."

The Routine

Kim was going to Spanish class, and Jared was on his way to French class. They would talk about Josh and Jason at lunch. The hallways were filled with almost 800 middle-school students, plus the teachers who have 9:50 A.M. hall duty and the school administrators who seem to always have hall duty. Jared spoke to some friends, but then turned away as some students started running in the hall toward a bathroom.

"What's up?" Jared asked Stephanie. "Why are those girls running so fast?"

"Oh, it's Ashley. She broke up with Craig. Big news," Stephanie explained.

"I thought they were really, you know, serious about each other. He gave her that ring and everything."

"Jared, here's what I heard. Craig went to a party Friday night when Ashley was out of town. The rumor is he could not keep his eyes off Carol. Ashley heard that and told Craig to get lost. Know what? It's not Craig's fault. Carol kept flirting with him. She hates Ashley."

"We gotta hurry. French starts in a few seconds."

"Talk to you later, Jared," Stephanie said as they took their seats in opposite corners of French class.

"Bonjour. Bonjour. Ça va?"

"Trés bien, monsieur le professeur, et vous?"

"Trés bien, merci. Ecoutez."

French class was all French all the time. No English was spoken. The students heard French, spoke French, thought French, and surrounded themselves with French culture. To be in this French class was to be in France. To be in this class was to experience the fascinating language, culture, and lifestyle of France.

Let's advance to the end of the school day. Jared will have attended five more classes—math, English, computer, physical education, and success. Success class is 20 minutes of one class period, and the other 30 minutes of that class period is lunch. Some teachers really use the 20 minutes for worthwhile and interesting activities that help middle-school students deal with typical situations, problems, or questions of 13-year-olds. Other teachers just say, "Do your homework" or "Talk quietly" while the teacher sits at his or her desk with some supposedly important tasks that must be done now.

During this day, Jared had some conversations with friends, some worksheets to complete, some interesting classes, and some boring classes. He caused no problems and got in no trouble. His B average is safe, and his clean behavior record is safe. He was late to one class, but that teacher never counts tardies because he is never ready to start class on time. The social studies class was the best, but basketball try-outs after school will evoke more energy and effort from Jared than all of today's classes combined. Jared is fascinated with basketball. Jared is tolerant of classes. Jared's basketball coach is more fascinated with basketball than with the subject he teaches. Jared's teachers range from Mr. Prather who is fascinated with social studies and who gets students interested in learning more than any teacher Jared ever saw to Ms. Armstrong who does little more than show up. How does all of this look to Jared? How would Jared describe a typical day or a typical year at school? He would say, "School is boring. It's just boring. We do the same stuff every day. You know, worksheets and chapters, multiple choice tests, or other tests, lots of listening to teachers, and too many math problems. Some teachers are cool, and their classes are OK. I like seeing my friends, and I really like basketball, but, you know, school is school. It's something you have to do. It's really boring."

DIFFERENT TEACHERS, SAME DUTY, DIFFERENT REACTIONS

Mr. Prather and Ms. Armstrong have adjacent parking spaces in the teachers' parking lot. On days they arrive at the same time, they chat while walking into the school. Ms. Armstrong usually starts the discussion with some complaint. That's what she did on this Monday morning at 7:36 A.M.

"Mr. Prather, did you see those students on the corner? They'll never pass their classes. I bet they skip school today."

"Ms. Armstrong, if they have your class, they should skip" was the response Mr. Prather wanted to make; instead he said, "Hey, let's go talk to them and be sure they come into the school."

"You can go talk to them. I have to copy some worksheets."

Some teachers copy worksheets at 7:40 A.M. Monday. Some teachers talk to students at 7:40 A.M. to be sure that those students come into the school, go to class, and do not skip school. For teachers whose career is dependent on the copy machine and worksheets, teaching is just a job, and school is boring. Those teachers make school boring for themselves and for students.

For teachers who see each student as one more opportunity for meaningful interaction, who see each student on a corner as one more opportunity to teach, who are more than ready for class so they can take advantage of a moment in which learning can be caused, teaching is fascinating, and school is life at its best.

Perhaps the difference between Ms. Armstrong and Mr. Prather is work ethic, yet more basic than that could be their perspective toward students. Ms. Armstrong "worksheets" and "chapters" her students. Mr. Prather interacts with his students. Ms. Armstrong sees students as lazy, apathetic, troublemakers with limited ability. Mr. Prather sees students as energetic, interesting people with unlimited ability. Ms. Armstrong assumes the worst and gets it. Ms. Prather seeks the best and often gets that, but always gets the satisfaction of a bold effort.

How would Ms. Armstrong describe a typical day at school?

"Oh, it's so busy. There is too much to do: meetings, schedules, lesson plans to complete, phone calls, papers to grade, discipline problems. It's all harder than it used to be. The students are different. I can retire in 5 years, and I hope I can last that long. We'll have a vacation soon, and that will help. School has just changed so much."

How would Mr. Prather describe a typical day at school?

"It is hard work, but I love it. I know that some students hate school and so do some teachers. I'm realistic. I know that some students steal, cheat, lie, and fight. I've just always thought that every student could learn and could behave, so I try to help each student be the best he or she can be. Part of that is being the best teacher I can be. The classroom should be lively and fascinating. The energy of students and their curiosity should be applied, not eliminated. I learn with the students. I'm in charge. I'm the adult. I'm the teacher, but I interact with the students. We learn together, and it really is fascinating."

SCHOOL PURPOSE

How would Jared, Ms. Armstrong, and Mr. Prather answer this question: What is the purpose of a school?

Jared: I guess the purpose of a school is to have a place for us to be during the day and to teach us. The real purpose of school is, like, you know, to keep us out of trouble. Where would all of us go if we did not have to go to school? It would be summer vacation all year. They tell us that school prepares us for a job. I guess that's part of the purpose.

Ms. Armstrong: Well, the purpose of a school is to educate the students according to the curriculum and the rules. Some parents seem to think that the purpose of school is to feed and supervise their children. I wonder what becomes of these children on weekends or in the summer. Who feeds them? Who watches them? School is also the place where a community employs its teachers. There is some efficiency in that plan instead of every family trying to educate their own children.

Mr. Prather: School is about learning and is about students. The purpose of a school is to make sure that every student learns all that he or she possibly can learn. This means that the people at school, especially teachers, have to cause learning. Students and parents or guardians have lots of responsibility in this, but teachers are the experts and should do whatever it takes—in legal, professional, and moral ways—to educate each student.

What is similar in those three answers? Do Jared, Ms. Armstrong, and Mr. Prather agree on the purpose of a school? About the only similarity is that school is a place where there are students and teachers, but as far as what those people are supposed to do, to be, and to become, there is no agreement from Jared and his two teachers. If there is no agreement on the purpose of a school, there will be serious limits on what is accomplished at that school.

SCHOOL IS BORING

Why didn't Jared and why wouldn't many students say, "School is cool. It's the place where each day is like an adventure. You explore ideas, and you think. You try new things, and you meet lots of people." To the readers who just said, "Get real, Keen," here is a response—children and teenagers could use those words to describe summer camp, a job, a scouting trip, a vacation, the sports team they play on, the marching band they are in, the church youth group car wash, the student council leadership workshop, or some classes at school. What prevents everything at school from getting an enthusiastic commitment from many students? Other wholesome, useful, practical, educational, helpful, constructive experiences of children and of teenagers do get rave reviews as do some classes. Why is much of school an experience that so many students merely endure? Because for those students *school is boring*.

For too many students in too many schools, too much time is spent in classrooms similar to Ms. Armstrong's. Ms. Armstrong is guilty of brain slaughter— she killed the students' interest in the solar system in particular and probably their interest in science in general.

Ms. Armstrong has her defenders who would offer comments such as

- "For some students, you just have to keep them busy and under control. Worksheets and reading a chapter are the best ways to teach those students. If you try something else, they'll just get out of control."
- "The textbook is supposed to be used. Ms. Armstrong would be criticized if she did not have the students read the textbook."
- "We've gotten too fancy in education. Let's get back to the basic procedures of doing drills such as worksheets and questions at the end of a chapter. Those worked years ago."

- "Ms. Armstrong probably has tried other teaching methods, but she knows what is best in her classroom for her students."
- "What's wrong with some old-fashioned, independent, silent study. Schools that try to amuse students will never get the job done. Don't expect Ms. Armstrong to be an entertainer. Learning is not always fun."
- "Ms. Armstrong has many years of service to the school system. Her performance reviews have always been satisfactory. The problem is these students. They just won't work. They expect school to be a party. Well, they are wrong."

The truth is that Ms. Armstrong is a classroom clerk. She is bored, and she is boring. She has infected her students with her boredom.

Many students are inherently interested in, if not fascinated by, the solar system. They want to know about stars, planets, space travels, and the possibilities of future space explorations. They have questions, curiosity, and wonder about space. The inherent fascination that children and teenagers have with space could be an essential part of magnificent learning in a classroom with a teacher who shares the students' fascination.

The students in Ms. Armstrong's classroom are bored by the solar system, by worksheets, by the textbook, and by the test. Ms. Armstrong could create solar system activities. Her room could become the universe with planets, the sun, and stars hanging from the ceiling and being moved occasionally. A short space exploration video could be shown. The history of space travel could be discussed. Students could interview their grandparents and parents about "Where were you in July 1969, when we got to the moon?" Newspaper accounts of that 1969 event could be read. A futuristic skit could be created to consider personal space travel. Instead, Ms. Armstrong has de-fascinated her students.

In a fascinating and fascinated classroom, the solar system and space could be discussed, explored, wondered about, and interacted with instead of worksheeted, textbooked, and multiple choiced. The solar system is fascinating. Learning about the solar system can be fascinating. All learning can be fascinating. To paraphrase Jerome Bruner's statement that "We can teach any subject to any student in an intellectually honest way," I would propose that "We can teach any subject to all students in an intellectually fascinating way."

Students have the right to be taught in a fascinating way by teachers who are fascinated with school, with learning, with teaching, and with students.

Students have the responsibility to make a complete effort to learn, to study, to cooperate, to participate, to follow rules, and to do all assignments well.

The best learning, the most fascinating learning, is a mutually accepted responsibility and a mutually experienced, interactive adventure.

Students—unless you are on time for school, on time for every class, prepared for every class, completing all homework on time, and as accurately as possible obeying school rules and paying total attention in class, you have no basis for any complaint about the teachers and the teaching. When you do conscientiously accept your duties and fulfill your responsibilities, you have earned the right to offer ideas, suggestions, and criticism.

Teachers—unless you demonstrate total commitment to and fascination with students, teaching, and learning, you have no basis for any complaint about students, parents, or school. Don't tell us about your lazy students or about their apathetic parents when you are late for class, suspiciously absent on Fridays, still using lesson plans from many years ago, showing videos to pass the time, not returning homework, distributing one more set of worksheets, and leaving the school building faster than the first exiting school bus.

Ms. Armstrong is obsolete. She has made herself obsolete. Any student can obtain the information Ms. Armstrong provides without coming into contact with Ms. Armstrong. Via books, libraries, computer software, computer on-line services, satellite transmission, television broadcasts, subscription services for printed or electronic materials, students can easily access the flat, collected bits of information that Ms. Armstrong has made a career of distributing to her students.

Ms. Armstrong really does function as a classroom clerk. She has chosen to reduce herself to that level. She assembles materials that a textbook publisher provided with the science book. If it is September 10, Ms. Armstrong copies pre-packaged worksheet #13 in a series of 100, which will culminate with worksheet #100 being copied one morning in May for students to complete a few days before the school year ends.

Ms. Armstrong uses other hand-outs that she has dutifully collected and accurately filed throughout her career. Ms. Armstrong collects a higher salary than many teachers because, in teaching, salary is a function of years of experience and college degrees. Ms. Armstrong is stealing from the taxpayers because she does not earn her pay, she is stealing from students who deserve a much better classroom experience, she is stealing from her colleagues who have to make up for what students are not given by Ms. Armstrong, and she is stealing from herself. Ms. Armstrong is denying herself a meaningful career and is denying herself the wonderful experiences that she and the students could adventurously share in the classroom.

In years past, Ms. Armstrong probably was a teacher instead of a classroom clerk. Maybe she is worn out or worn down. Maybe the years of work in school absorbed her idealism, energy, and creativity. Maybe personal or family problems are a burden. Maybe she was never great at teaching and should not have been hired or re-hired years ago. Those speculations are not the issue and are not excuses.

Ms. Armstrong is employed to cause learning. She can be shown how to cause learning. She can be supported, observed, trained, and guided, but she is responsible for results. Her students deserve results. Teaching is for students, not for teachers. Schools are for students, not for teachers.

Students who enter Ms. Armstrong's classroom or any middle-school or high-school classroom on a typical Monday morning are people who spent the prior weekend involved in a broad variety of experiences. Some used their home computers to communicate throughout the electronic global village. Some participated in sports, church activities, social events, or personal hobbies. Some were active in wholesome family activities while some battled with, evaded, or were ignored by their families. Some had part-time jobs. Some participated in extra-curricular school events. Some studied seriously, and others never gave school a thought. Some broke laws and were caught. Some gathered in gangs or in groups that looked and sounded like gangs. Some just wasted time. Some watched endless television.

For almost every student who enters a classroom on Monday morning, the teacher can assume that whatever those students did for the past 65 hours—from high-technology computer processing to low-life juvenile crime—they probably see little connection between what will happen in class and what matters to them.

The adults establish the curriculum and the rules. The adults decide how school operates. The duty of the adults will not be reduced; however, in accepting the idea that the purpose of school is to cause learning, the adults at school can give themselves the advantage of using methods and materials that matter to students. Come on, reading one more Charles Dickens book can be an utterly meaningless task of enduring words on a page—unless, the teacher makes the study of Dickens' ideas an intense exploration of what it is like to be a teenager in a nation where poverty is increasing, the gap in rich and poor living standards is increasing, and government leaders seem baffled by existing conditions. Is that a description of Dickens' era or today? The discussion could be fascinating.

It is the responsibility of a conscientious teacher to show students how the education being obtained through school is worthwhile today, now, right here in the lives of students. Making the educational content meaningful while also making the teaching methods and the classroom experiences fascinating can help convince students to commit their energies and abilities to learning at school. This may also awaken some currently hibernating or excuse-making teachers who can rediscover the bold adventure of actually teaching, of actually causing learning.

LEARNING IS FASCINATING

Children and young people learn constantly. In their younger years, they always ask questions. Adults can encourage this curiosity, or adults can smother that curiosity. Students who are encouraged to ask, to wonder, to explore, and whose natural inclination to find out why and how is supported can become students who never tire of inquiry, of thought, of learning.

Listen to the conversations of young people. You will hear questions and comments that show an eagerness to know. For example: (1) "How'd they do that chase scene in that movie?" The answer could be part of a great science, math, or computer lesson. (2) "How do you hit three-point shots?" The answer could be part of a memorable lesson on physics, fitness, and math. (3) "How do I drive a car?" Every topic from language (traffic signs) to history (various means of transportation) to math and science could be part of the total answer. (4) "How do I make some money?" Certainly, math could be part of this discussion, but so could integrity, honesty, discipline, work ethic, and saving.

Children constantly say, "Let me do it." They are eager to learn by doing or to do by learning.

Young people learn from television, music, each other, and anyone or anything they trust, like, think is real, or believe is important.

So, why don't children and teenagers learn as much as adults try to teach them in school? Of the many reasons, there is one that students have included in my discussions with them for 15 years when I asked them why they did not work harder in school or why they did not take school more seriously: "School is boring." No student ever told me that learning is boring; they told me that school is boring.

Intensity

I would then ask students why they did get interested in other parts of school life such as sports, band, field trips, and clubs or why they got excited about amusement parks, movies, or going out for pizza? The answers from students can be summarized in one word—intensity.

I'm a good teacher, and frequently I have been a great teacher. Why? The students tell me it is because "You make it interesting. You don't just have us read the book or fill in sheets. You make it matter to us. You involve us."

When I teach, the purpose of my work is to cause learning by creating an intensity, a vibrant drama in the classroom. The intensity creates interest, attention, responses, interaction, curiosity, thinking, and learning. Drama is a major part of this intellectual intensity and instructional intensity. Theater, energy, imagination, creativity, performances, scripts, rehearsals, props, ideas, excitement, communication, silence, and surprises. Intensity. Drama. Live performances of human beings encountering ideas, interacting with those ideas, and interacting with each other result in fascination and learning.

The idea for intense, dramatic, creative human intellectual interaction as a foundation for and a method of fascinating teaching was shown to this writer during many years by several superior teachers. In my junior high, senior high, college, and graduate school experiences, there were seven teachers whose classrooms were more vibrant and thrilling than any Hollywood special effects, amusement park roller coaster, or bottom-of-the-ninth-inning game-winning grand slam home run. These teachers were so fascinated with their subjects, with their students, with learning, with causing learning, and with the adventure of teaching that students reciprocated with genuine fascination with learning. The result was learning!

There were no excuses. Society was not blamed. Lazy students were not blamed. Dysfunctional families, television, education reform, liberals, conservatives, broken copy machines, budgets, apathy, or laziness were not blamed. The classroom experiences provided by and the total learning experiences inspired by these teachers were fascinating and the students, despite any other original inclination, worked harder, cooperated more, learned more, and for part of their education knew the pure goodness and joy of thinking and of learning

Standards

If other teachers can fascinate their students, why aren't all teachers fascinating all of their students all of the time? Almost all teachers this author has known wanted their students to learn, wanted to inspire their students, and wanted those students to be committed to school; however, some of those teachers have grown weary of angry parents, endless meetings, or other realities that sap energy. A few of those teachers may be "doing their time" until retirement, but most teachers still have high hopes and deep convictions about the success of each student.

The skeptics and cynics are shouting back, "Every teacher fascinating all students all of the time—that is impossible. That's too idealistic. No way."

Those same skeptics and cynics will tolerate a drop-out rate and a failure rate in schools, but they expect their doctors to always be accurate in a diagnosis and treatment, their pharmacists to always be accurate in filling a prescription, their mechanics to always be accurate in repairing their cars, the traffic engineers to always have every stop light functioning correctly, and the grocery to always have every item on their food list.

Imagine going to a restaurant where 65% of the meals are properly served, but the other 35% are just empty plates. Too bad. Your plate is empty, but you still owe the money, plus a tip. Hey, according to school standards, the restaurant's grade is passing.

Imagine that 65% of the time people report a fire, the fire department arrives. The other 35% of the time, the building is left to burn. In schools, that 65% would be a passing grade.

What do a school's basketball players do when 2 minutes are left in the game? They work. Their intensity increases. The coach instructs. Interaction increases. Nobody quits until the final second ticks away. The coach is expected to get total commitment from each athlete always.

What happens in many school classrooms a few minutes before the bell rings? People give up. Books are closed. Minds are emptied. It's over. Why waste the final 2 minutes? Aren't 2 classroom minutes as precious as 2 basketball minutes?

We know what works in schools. We know what does not work. Some new laws or new taxes may help, but higher standards, a stronger work ethic, and some fascinating teaching can also start some progress.

Coaches are not satisfied if most athletes know nine out of ten plays. Every player has to know every play. Band directors are not satisfied if most musicians play nine out of ten notes correctly. Every person plays every note of every song correctly, or you repeat it until that standard is reached.

We know what causes learning: hard work, books, studying, tests, reading, memorizing, enthusiasm, rewards, thinking, asking questions, activities, relating students' experiences to today's lessons, writing, interaction, simulations, exploring, expressing opinions, working with a group, conducting research individually, applying information, and a fascinated and fascinating teacher.

There is a valid question that capable, competent, hard-working, frustrated, exhausted, and determined teachers ask: "I've done all of that. I use every creative, dynamic, and energetic teaching method ever invented. I give the students choices and options. We work in groups. I offer rewards. No matter what I do, some students, maybe 5% or 10%, never respond. That group has already decided that they will fail my class and probably most of their other classes. What else can I do?"

The idealistic response is that every student is interested in something. There are many heroic stories of a determined teacher who discovered that a disruptive, failing student had one interest in life. The interest could be music, money, sports, cars, movies, karate, motorcycles, bicycles, clothes, or other topics. From one teacher who built upon the student's interest in music, other teachers were persuaded to let this student structure a science project about music, a history report about music, a language arts project presented as a music video, and a math assignment done to show the relationship between notes and numbers. The student started passing classes, attending school regularly, and behaving better. The student was not making straight A's, having perfect attendance, and avoiding all misbehavior, but progress was being made. It can happen.

Reality Check

The answer that reflects a current reality is that today's student body does have a percentage of students who have already written off school. For these students, school is a convenient collection of people to steal from, sell drugs to, assault, harass, or defy. These students need to be educated in facilities that are in the "alternative" category. These facilities will range from 24-hour juvenile detention centers for court involved offenders to highly supervised, highly structured, alternative schools where teachers, school security, social workers, probation officers, school psychologists, and school counselors work intensely with students.

To admit that 5% to 10% of students cannot or will not succeed in the standard school setting is merely an honest acknowledgment. The 90% to 95% of students who can succeed in the standard school setting deserve to pursue their education without the disruptions that happen when one school tries to be everything to everyone. The 5% to 10% of students who need an alternative school setting deserve to be educated effectively. It is possible that this smaller group could someday realize that learning in school is fascinating. They already know that learning is fascinating, but what they have been learning—crime, dishonesty, violence, defiance—and where they have learned it—on the streets, from criminals, from family members—is a dead end for them and for their communities. Please notice that although what those students learned on the streets is destructive or deadly or illegal, they did make the effort to learn. Were they in awe of the new car a drug dealer drove? Were they impressed with the stolen property that some thieves had? Did they just want to be in on some action with people who accepted them even if the action was immoral or illegal and if the acceptance was superficial and fleeting?

Every young person is interested in something, but for many children and teenagers—not just the currently incorrigible 5% to 10%—school is increasingly dismissed as something they just have to get through. These are the same young people who will attend twice-a-day sports practices, memorize the schedule to television programs, spend hours of total concentration mastering a new video game, who can easily fly through the internet to have e-mail chats, and who will do anything to learn how to drive a car. Schools cannot base the curriculum solely on the current interests of students; however, (1) those interests can complement instruction, which will cause the students to learn the curriculum, and (2) the fact that the students have interests confirms that they are fascinated with something and, therefore, are "fascinate-able" people who could join a fascinating teacher in the adventure of learning at school.

A School Culture of Fascination

Imagine this possibility—making school a learning place with many daily experiences that fascinate students, that cause students to learn, that cause teachers to also learn and to experience career satisfaction, and that create a school culture of "we are in this together" as everyone works toward reaching the school's purpose. By doing this, teachers and students can team up in the fascinating adventure of learning, rather than battle each other in the frustrating war of teachers trying to get students to do what they should do and students trying to get out of doing what they should do.

The key factor in creating a fascinating school is creating fascinating classroom experiences. Students spend most of their school hours, days, and years under the authority of a teacher. The pivotal power in education is exercised in classrooms; therefore, creating fascinating experiences in the classroom can help make school a place where learning occurs and where students are fascinated. These experiences will include some vital ingredients that help create compelling interaction between (1) the students and the teacher and (2) the students, the teacher, and a topic, activity, lesson, or idea.

INTERACTION

These experiences will bring elements of creativity, high energy, academics, unexpected methods, traditional methods, imagination, and intensity to cause *interaction*—between people, between people and ideas, between ideas and ideas—that fascinates students and that helps cause learning. These experiences include conditions and components that teachers can provide while also including clear responsibilities for students.

Consider the aphorism, "Truth emerges when ideas collide." As ideas compete in an intellectual democracy, truth will emerge. For schools, the aphorism could be modified: "Learning occurs when ideas, experiences, and people interact." The Interaction Lesson Plan—Basic Concept below provides step 1 of a process that can help teachers design lessons that fascinate students, cause interaction, are intense, and cause learning.

INTERACTION LESSON PLAN—BASIC CONCEPT
This lesson will cause learning:

a. Of this idea, information, or skill _____

b. Through these activities _____

c. With this interaction _____
   (includes students, teachers, and materials)
d. Learning will be measured by and confirmed by this method _____

For example:

a. Of this idea: Calculating unit costs will enable a consumer to make a wise decision.
b. Through this activity: Students will be shown (1) an actual size cardboard pizza that is 20" long and 12" wide and (2) two actual size cardboard pizzas that are 12" in diameter. The students will be given the prices from five different pizza restaurants for their rectangular and round pizzas. Students will work individually to make all calculations and then in pairs to decide (3) which option is more economical at each restaurant and (4) which restaurant has the best deal on pizza.
c. With this interaction: Students will work in pairs as stated above and will then work in groups of four to six to create a commercial for a pizza restaurant. Each restaurant will have one group making a commercial, which will be presented/acted.
d. Learning will be confirmed and measured by: (1) The math calculations will be checked by the teacher. (2) Homework will be a one-page answer to this: "How to be a smart pizza buyer." (3) The teacher and the students will discuss the pizza pricing and the content of the commercials. (4) A pizza restaurant manager will visit the class tomorrow to answer questions from students, to interview the students as prospective employees, and to serve pizza.

The Interaction Lesson Plan—Basic Concept is step 1 and enables teachers to think through the general flow of a lesson. The Interaction Lesson Plan—Instruction Grid shown in Chapter 3 is step 2 and provides a more specific implementation tool that can help teachers tap innovative combinations of materials and experiences to increase and improve interaction. That chapter will provide details on how to create fascinating lessons.

Of course, the teacher could have put a few examples of math problems on the board to show how the area of a rectangle is calculated and then to show how the area of a circle is calculated. The teacher could then say, "Any questions? OK, for tomorrow, do the even problems on page 142, numbers 2 through 36. Show your work. Start now, please." Which lesson is more fascinating? Which lesson could cause more learning—the pizza lesson or the textbook lesson? Yes, some standard work on rectangle and circle area is needed, but applying that information and interacting with that information can build fascination, which helps cause learning, which helps build commitment to learning, which helps reduce boredom and its related problems.

Why is interaction so important? A big portion of life itself is the sum of human interaction. Here's a simple example: contrast going to a movie alone versus going to a movie with a friend. If you went alone, you silently watched the film, and as you returned home, you gave it some thought, but until someone says to you, "Did you see that new movie about the teacher?" and you discuss it, you will not fully experience the content of or the impact of the film.

If you went to the movie with a friend, you probably discussed reviews of the film, you had some whispered comments during the movie—"Why did he say that to her?" or "What do you think will happen next?"—and you discussed the movie as you left the theater. Which experience of the movie was more meaningful and more memorable? Which experience was enhanced by the perspective of another person who enabled you to realize something in the film that you had not particularly noticed. Which experience was more fascinating?

Yes, people can learn alone. People can read a book, write a report, watch a film, listen to a tape, or complete a worksheet alone and begin to learn something, but that learning is limited. It is through interacting with other people who also read the book, wrote a report, watched the film, listened to the tape, or completed the worksheet that meaning, purpose, application, extension, and understanding can be added to the initial awareness and learning.

Think again about the movie theater and the movie industry. The people who make Hollywood happen know how to totally surround customers with information about, souvenirs from, and experiences with movies. "Previews of coming attractions," movie-related toys given free with purchase of a meal at certain restaurants, clothing with movie characters, contests on radio stations giving away tickets to the premiere of the movie, and short clips from the movie sent to television stations for use in a "What to do this weekend" story all help create the fascination people have with movies. How could Hollywood's fascinating methods be applied in schools?

Teachers can give students previews of upcoming lessons. Students could be involved in creating and in presenting the previews. A school can have its mascot, name, and/or logo printed on anything from keychains to T-shirts. A local radio station could team-up with a school so well-known radio personalities tape record some of the school's announcements, which are then played on the school's public address system. School events can be videotaped and broadcast on the local cable television system. Posters can cover the walls of the school. These student creations could communicate any subject from school rules to the most recent "Students of the Week." The result could be some new excitement at school and the creation of a culture of fascination at school.

One final reality check—great teaching is hard work. Being a continually fascinating teacher whose classroom is constantly fascinating to children and teenagers is exhausting. It is harder work, and it is more exhausting to teach poorly. Boring, ineffective teaching leads to extra work as more students misbehave and become discipline cases, as more students fail and need remedial programs, as more students drop out and disrupt communities, as more teachers complain about their jobs and poison the attitudes or work environment of their colleagues, and as teachers just give up, quit, retire, or stay at school and merely go through the motions of being a teacher.

For students and for teachers, creating fascinating lessons, classrooms, and schools brings education alive, builds commitment to learning, and helps build a shared sense of purpose about school. As teachers, when we chose teaching as our career and/or when teaching chose us, our intentions included being the kind of teacher who really got through to the students, who really inspired the students, who challenged successful students to learn more, who encouraged the average student to improve, and who inspired the failing student to work. When teachers begin their teaching career, it is usually with the intention of being fascinated and fascinating. This book is intended (1) as a reminder of the original promises teachers made to themselves, (2) as a "how to" interactive book to show good teachers how to be even more fascinating, to show struggling teachers how to recapture fascination, and to show future teachers how to implement their dreams, (3) as an acknowledgment that if learning does not occur, teaching did not occur, and (4) as an antidote to the fact that although learning is fascinating, for too many students, school is boring.

In the next chapter, the reasons for and the methods of making schools places where fascinating learning occurs will be further explored. We are in this together—teachers and students. Let's team up to fascinate ourselves and each other. First, some encouraging words:

WE KNOW WHAT WORKS

There is no reason to be timid or confused.

There is no reason to doubt or to give up.

There is no reason to worry or to complain.

There is every reason to be confident and to be convinced.

There is every reason to be optimistic and to be determined.

There is every reason to strive, to work, to dream, and to hope.

We know what works.

We know how to make a difference. We know how to change.

We know how to adventurously plan and to courageously achieve.

We know how to improve and to revise and to build.

We know what works.

An attitude that says, "We'll find a way."

An ability to plan, to anticipate, and to prepare.

The persistence and the energy to never give up.

The wisdom to ask for advice and to use the advice given.

The knowledge that we cannot go it alone and that we do not have to go it alone.

The acceptance of mistakes and the maturity to do better next time.

The courage to try, to care, to love, to hope, and to have faith.

We know what works.

Enough sleep, the right food, some exercise, reading good books, discipline, time management, goal setting, sharing, listening, work, thinking, team building, taking a walk, high standards, more work.

We know what fails.

Fatigue, junk, laziness, chaos, wasted time, talking too much, goofing off, having nothing to aim at, wild extremes, drugs, immorality, crime, bad manners, stupidity, never changing.

There is every reason to live vibrantly, to care deeply, to hope endlessly, to believe mightily, and to work tirelessly.

We know what works, and we know that we can do it, so let's go on the adventure of making a difference for good in the lives of students. With faith, hope, and love, we shall persist.

CHAPTER 3

Interaction Between Students and Teachers Builds Fascinating Schools

If learning did not occur, teaching did not occur. When the education profession accepts that standard, there will be a potential for increased support and trust from the public. When the adults at a school always exemplify the behavior, work ethic, and commitment to school that is expected of students, there can be some wonderful results as students follow those commendable examples.

Most teachers have attended meetings, training sessions, or professional development workshops that were painfully dull and that were completely unproductive; however, many of those teachers subject their students to equally dull experiences in their classrooms. Again, if the adults set the example, the students are likely to follow.

The movie *Field of Dreams* used this idea. "If you build it, they will come." The parallel in teaching is, "If you fascinate students, they will learn."

This chapter builds upon a qualitative survey to further develop a method for creating and implementing lessons that fascinate teachers and students, that foster interaction, that build intensity, and that cause learning.

WE are in this together means that teachers and students need to team up in the adventure of learning. It also means that what happens in schools has an immediate and long-term impact throughout our communities and our society. There are many people who are willing to offer ideas, time, work, and resources to helping schools accomplish more and become more fascinating places where much meaningful learning is caused.

THE EDUCATIONAL IMPERATIVE

A May 1996 qualitative survey conducted by the author provides ideas from twenty such people. Participants in the survey included the following, among others: a corporate vice-president from a Fortune 500 company

35

(actually the company is among the twenty largest in the nation), a police officer, a medical doctor, a prison warden, a college president, a graduate-school professor, two college students, presidents of two small businesses, an educator at the state government level, a high-school teacher, a marketing research director, and a newspaper reporter. These people provided thoughtful insight that will be detailed on the following pages; however, one dominant theme emerged from each respondent—never has education been more urgently needed! Years ago, a television commercial used the slogan "To get a good job, get a good education," and that idea seemed to be true. The idea that emerges with urgency from the respondents to the author's qualitative survey is "To live a good life, get a good educational foundation that will enable you to earn a living and to keep learning for a lifetime."

There are more challenges, problems, and opportunities now than ever before, and our communities, states, and nation seem to be relying on improved education. The assumption is that education is the most effective method available to develop human skills, abilities, and knowledge, which can enable people to confront challenges, problems, and opportunities. At stake is more than the economic competitiveness of the United States, although that is part of the urgency. At stake is whether our society has peaked and faces a future of decline or whether our third century as a nation can surpass the prior 200 years in how we treat each other, in how we create opportunities, in how we maintain secure and peaceful communities, in how civil our public debates are, in how honorable our political process is, in how we rear our children, in how we care for our elderly, in how we manage our finances, in how we preserve our environment, and in how we function as a democratic, capitalistic country.

Our society expects education to be the foundation upon which we correct problems, prevent problems, direct lives, and build the future. Never have the stakes for education been so high. Never has our nation asked so much of education. Never has it been more important to create schools in which every classroom each day is a place where learning is caused as teachers and students interact in fascinating, meaningful, and purposeful ways. We seem to face an education imperative—successfully educate all students or become a second-rate society.

SURVEY RESULTS

The qualitative survey included three questions. The first question was "What do students need to know by the time they graduate from high school? Once it was reading, writing, and arithmetic—what is it now?" A representative sample of answers follows:

- "Computer skills, manners, and respect for themselves."
- "Those basics plus a lot more. [They] must be prepared to constructively participate in community, culture, government, and commerce, be prepared for higher education, or be vocationally prepared to earn a living."
- "Basic grammar and reasoning skills—decent articulation, ability to communicate orally and verbally; a strong sense of history."
- "Basic skills in reading and writing, ability to retrieve and then apply relevant information as needed; some orientation to social sciences, the arts, literature."
- "Computer skills—e-mail, internet, world wide web."
- "Need better grammar skills, problem solving, basic math."
- "How to communicate, which means being able to speak and write correctly."
- "Communication skills are a must. The knowledge of how to operate computers is a must."
- "Students need to have a well-rounded education."
- "They need to be capable of learning."
- "Reading, writing, and arithmetic are still the key basics. Beyond these basics, there is an increasing requirement for reasoning, for what is often called critical thinking skills, and for some fundamental values such as respect and timeliness."

These comments emphasize six essential skills for students to acquire including the basics of reading, writing, and arithmetic:

(1) Basics: reading, writing, and arithmetic
(2) Communication
(3) Computer use
(4) Thinking/reasoning
(5) Problem solving
(6) Learning how to learn

The second question on the survey was "What skills do students need to acquire if they are going to be ready to succeed in a job with your company or organization? Some representative responses are below:

- "People skills, problem-solving skills, communication skills."
- "Must be a life-long learner."
- "A strong sense of civility and respect for the other person."
- "Capacity to think critically and articulate ideas; increasingly, some sense of computer skills."

- "Work habits regarding dependability; ability to learn continuously and transfer previous learning to new job demands and responsibilities."
- "Computer skills, common sense, a sense of what business is, creative skills."
- "Willingness to learn, ability to get along with co-workers."
- "Ability to write, to communicate with many people, to reason and problem solve, to listen and synthesize information."
- "Intangible things, such as attitude, punctuality, and work ethic."
- "Students need to have the skill to communicate intelligently in the English language and to perform basic math tasks with understanding. They must have the skills to operate a personal computer."
- "A strong work ethic. Also, it is increasingly important to be able to work both independently and as part of a team."

Note: Many respondents repeated that fundamental reading, writing, and arithmetic skills were basic essentials on the job.

Questions 1 and 2 are similar. The responses are similar, but responses to question 2 added skills that enable a person to apply his or her ability on the job site. The question 2 comments above emphasize seven essential on-the-job skills shown below:

(1) Communication: write, speak, listen

(2) Computer use

(3) Thinking

(4) Problem solving

(5) Life-long learning

(6) People skills including listening and working as a team

(7) Work ethic including being dependable and punctual

Based on these responses to Questions 1 and 2, students need to master eight skills: (1) reading, writing, arithmetic, (2) communication, (3) computers, (4) thinking, (5) problem solving, (6) learning how to learn, (7) becoming people who can work cooperatively with other people, and (8) having a strong work ethic. What can schools and teachers do to cause students to learn these important skills and other vital skills? The responses to Question 3 offer some ideas. Question 3 was "(A) What did your best teachers do to make learning fascinating? (B) What can schools do now to build student interest in, commitment to, and fascination with learning?"

Representative responses to part A of Question 3 are below:

- "My best teachers were firm, had high expectations, were consistent, challenged me, and appeared to value me as I was."

- "Used a multi-media approach: textbook, audio, video, demonstration, class participation."
- "Created ways to organize required learning as an adventure; utilized active learning strategies rather than relying on passive learning."
- "Classroom discussion; case studies; Socratic question and answer learning."
- "Got students to set goals and associated the learning with how it would help students reach their goals."
- "Inspired a love of reading."
- "Used a variety of strategies and techniques—not just lecture, notes, questions at the end of the chapter. Challenged students to find the solution and to apply the knowledge."
- "Taught with enthusiasm and with some degree of passion about their subject."
- "Helped students understand how the learning was relevant to their lives."
- "My best teachers never told me what I couldn't do—they simply helped me find ways to achieve."
- "My own best teachers provided stimulating challenges. I had a high-school English teacher who, when we walked into the classroom for the final exam, simply went up to the blackboard and wrote WRITE and sat down. Half of the students just stared at the board for 10 minutes, while the rest of us scrambled to come up with something meaningful."

Representative responses to part B of Question 3 are below:

- "High expectation of teacher performance in maintaining a learning environment."
- "The most important thing is the role model. When students see an excited teacher, they tend to capture that sense of excitement."
- "Create the circumstances whereby students clearly understand the connections between their living situations and what they learn."
- "Focus on discussion rather than lecture. Tap student input by encouraging participation."
- "Show them the best; read them the best; expose them to the best."
- "Connect past learning with new knowledge acquisition. Use a variety of strategies, traditional and nontradition, to connect learning with real-life and meaningful situations."
- "If a student has a wrong answer, a teacher should not shoot him or her down, but should help the student understand why it is wrong in a nondefensive way."

The major ideas from the responses to both parts of Question 3 are itemized below:

(1) Challenge students; set high expectations for students and for teachers.

(2) Use a variety of teaching methods or strategies with emphasis on active involvement of students.

(3) Be enthusiastic; offer much encouragement.

(4) Connect learning with students' lives now in their real world.

Simply stated, these respondents are suggesting that teachers and students interact meaningfully, energetically, and actively with each other and with the curriculum to create purposeful, challenging, learning experiences. Sounds fascinating! The rectangle versus circle pizza activity would meet the standards cited above. Making school fascinating includes making school challenging, using a variety of active teaching methods, being enthusiastic, offering encouragement, and connecting learning with the real lives students are living now in their real world and with all of life in the total real world.

If thousands of people were surveyed about the same questions this author used, those results may have much in common with the replies of the people cited previously. Educators, business leaders, political leaders, or community leaders would probably agree that schools need to equip students with (1) basic academic skills plus skills in (2) communication, (3) computer use, (4) thinking, (5) problem solving, and (6) preparation for life-long learning. Few people would oppose those goals even if they added other goals, such as (7) solid people skills and (8) a strong work ethic.

If we can generally agree that the purpose of a school is to cause learning and that the learning should include, but not be limited necessarily to, the eight items cited in the paragraph above, why is it so difficult to get students interested in mastering those skills and why is it so difficult to get all teachers to teach in ways that sufficiently fascinate students to inspire them or to convince them to learn?

That is not the issue raised in this book. Other authors will study the varied motivations of great, average, and weak teachers. Other authors will study the varied motivations of successful, average, and unsuccessful students.

SCHOOL IS BORING; LEARNING IS FASCINATING

This book accepts the premise that education has never been more important; however, despite the unprecedented importance of education, many students have this perspective toward education: (1) school is boring although (2) learning is fascinating. There is a massive disconnect among school reformers, educators, students, and society. It is the hope of this author that the fascinating school and the fascinating classroom can be a method, "the how," that helps implement the curriculum, goals, and purpose, "the what and the why," of a school. Students who do not find fascination at school will look elsewhere to satisfy their youthful curiosities and energies.

Recall that Jerome Bruner has told us that anything can be taught to any student in an intellectually honest way. The next step can be the teaching frontier that says that "We can teach anything to any student in an intellectually fascinating way." If some students are already doing well, imagine how much better they could do in a fascinating school. Students doing poorly may be inspired to improve in a fascinating school. OK, it sounds good, but how is it done?

Think differently. School is not merely textbooks, worksheets, schedules, meetings, and report cards. School is people—real people living real lives, students included. School is a place where real people of all ages can interact in meaningful, purposeful, genuine, sincere ways to create an atmosphere, a culture, a constant experience of the fascination that is learning.

School is not a vacation, a party, a playground, or an all-day social event. School is a place where learning is to be caused, and that means much hard work is necessary; however, school also is the place where imaginations, innovations, debates, discussion, experiments, and creativity can explore the known and the currently unknown.

Fascination Can Happen

Are all students constantly fascinated with and by learning at school now? No. Are all teachers constantly fascinated with and by causing learning at school for all students now? No. Is it possible to create schools with a culture of fascination? It has to be possible. Learning itself is fascinating. Schools, places where learning is caused, can and must be fascinating places. How is this done? Part of the answer is to unplug the copy machine so dull, ordinary worksheets cannot be copied. Throw away the materials prepared by publishers of textbooks. Discard previously used lesson plans. Put the textbooks on the shelf for occasional use. Now think of the greatest teachers you had when you were in school and of the greatest teachers you have known during your career. What do these people know about teaching and what do they do?

They are enthusiastic, creative, unpredictable, imaginative, serious, humorous, determined, and invigorating. They interact with students. They use each second of time in class. They cause learning.

Please note, these great teachers had different personalities. Great teaching, fascinating teaching is not a function of one particular personality type. There are many ways to be fascinating, and there are many ways to be boring. It may help to be outgoing, but even a naturally shy person can do what outgoing people do. Even a teacher who uses worksheets daily can change the activity from another worksheet about planets to making models of planets. The activity in the classroom can change, and the bored and boring teacher may catch the excitement of learning and start to be more energetic.

In teaching business, I once asked students to create a new breakfast cereal. Each student had to design the box, name the product, present a commercial for the product, and convince us that this was the best cereal in the world. They did better work than some current cereal companies. They learned more about business than any book, worksheet, or lecture could have taught. This activity had some drama, some imagination, some relevance, much interaction, and much learning.

Fascinating teaching is not about fun. Fascinating teaching is about fascination; this is not about fleeting amusements, but about intellectual adventures. This is not about relying only on the current interests of students as the foundation of a teaching method or as the basis of a curriculum; yet, this does build upon and use students' interests as one resource in the endeavor to commit students to the fascination of learning in school.

The adults are in charge, but the students become more involved by their interactive participation in learning. The fascinating teacher teaches with students doing more than passive gazing, note taking, filling in blanks, or circling one of the multiple choices. Yes, some school processes are rather direct, and some notes do need to be taken in class, but school can be so much more than that because real, complete, meaningful learning is so much more than that.

Fascinating teaching is all of the drama of life itself, coupled with the limitless thoughts of the human mind and all of the constant energy of young people. Fascinating teaching is consistent with a high standard of educational accountability, which says that "If learning did not occur, teaching did not occur." Teachers with a year's supply of worksheets may be busy people, but they are not necessarily causing learning. Teachers should measure themselves by how much teaching they did, which means how much learning they caused, not by how many copy machines they exhausted.

The adults at school are in charge. The adults will not remove all rules and responsibilities for students and tell them "go do what you want to do, go do what fascinates you." Rather, the adults live what they expect the students to live. The adults exemplify what they expect the students to do, to be, and to become. The ways the adults at school teach and interact with each other and with students demonstrate what and how the students are expected to learn.

For example, recall what the survey respondents indicated that students need to know when they graduate from high school so they can be prepared for successful careers in work and/or in additional education:

(1) Basics—reading, writing, and arithmetic

(2) Communication

(3) Computer use

(4) Thinking

(5) Problem solving

(6) Life-long learning

7) People skills

(8) Work ethic

Are the adults in schools constantly demonstrating, exemplifying, and advancing personally in those eight skills? How could a teacher, administrator, student, or parent check to see if a classroom or a total school is constantly exemplifying and implementing those eight skills? The Interaction Lesson Plan—Instruction Grid shown in Figure 3.1 can help. This grid combines (a) survey results indicating the eight skills students need to master

	Teacher Skills			
	A Challenge Students	**B** Variety of Teaching Methods	**C** Enthusiasm & Encourage- ment	**D** Connect Learning with Living
Student Skills				
1. Basics				
2. Communication				
3. Computer Use				
4. Thinking				
5. Problem Solving				
6. Life-long Learning				
7. People Skills				
8. Work Ethic				

Figure 3.1.   Interaction Lesson Plan—Instruction Grid.

(pages 37–38, 40) with (b) the four teacher skills that the survey respondents emphasized (page 40). Details are on page 43.

This grid takes the skills that have been identified as essential for high-school graduates plus the components of fascinating teaching and creates an eight by four chart with thirty-two cells. Following use of the Interaction Lesson Plan—Basic Concept form on pages 30–31, the grid can be used as step 2 by a teacher to more specifically design a lesson plan, a unit, a grading period, a school year, or a curriculum. The grid also helps a teacher check a lesson's basic concept for interaction opportunities. "OK, I know the lesson is about the Bill of Rights and will use case studies. Is there a way to use computers? Am I using enough variety of teaching methods?" The basic concept form and the grid could be used by a principal to assess teachers, lesson plans, instruction, curriculum, and the school culture. The basic concept form and the grid could be used by sponsors of extra-curricular activities to guide the learning that can come from a well-designed club and sports activity program. The grid can be used by parents or guardians to evaluate a school. The grid can be used by a school renewal/reform/transformation team as one instrument used to help determine current conditions at a school.

Please note, there is no intention here to become bureaucratic or to cause complications. So far, we have explored two steps in the Interaction Lesson Plan process: Step 1 is to *develop the basic concept* of the lesson; step 2 is to specifically *design the instruction* of the lesson so teachers use effective skills to develop skills in students. We'll get to step 3 soon—that step emphasizes the sequence for activities that implement the basic concept and the instruction.

How is the instruction grid implemented? Consider cell 1A, which is the intersection of basic skills (for the purposes of this book, basic skills will include reading, writing, and arithmetic) and challenging students. A teacher using this grid asks herself or himself, "How do I design a lesson that strengthens a basic skill while also challenges the students?" A basic skill lesson that is not challenging would be unacceptable. The Chapter 1 pizza lesson provided opportunities for learning and applying some basic math skills while also challenging students to think, problem solve, and use people skills in their work group; used a variety of teaching methods—pencil and paper for arithmetic calculations, working alone, working in a group, making a presentation to the class—and connected the arithmetic to the real-life procedure of purchasing pizza. Student skills 1, 2, 4, 5, and 7 were used, and teacher skills A, B, and D were used in this pizza lesson, actually lesson*s* because it would continue for a few days.

In a fascinating classroom, the question is not "What is the teacher having the students do?" or "What is the teacher doing to the students?"; rather, the question is "What are the teacher and the students doing together to cause learning?"

Reality check—the pizza lesson is built upon very effective and very precise direct instruction of how to calculate the area of a rectangle and how to calculate the area of a circle. The teacher does teach, perhaps in a very traditional in-front-of-the-class way of presenting ideas, questions, and information, as part of a lesson or unit. The teacher conveys genuine fascination with the process of calculating area. The teacher shares a 3-minute account of the invention/discovery of Pi. The teacher communicates pure fascination with each student and with the interaction that Socratic questioning as part of direct instruction can provide.

The teacher continually interacts with individual students as they do their pencil and paper calculations. "Check your multiplication on this" or "Great work—keep it up" or "Is that the right length and width or did some numbers get mixed up?" The teacher listens to the groups of students and interjects provocative, guiding questions. The teacher may occasionally say, "Let's all listen for a moment. Several groups are getting confused about the final calculation for unit pricing. Let's review that. What's the information you need to determine a unit price?"

Rubric (Grading Guide)

The teacher provides a rubric for the commercials that will be created so students know what must be included for a superior commercial and what would cause a commercial to be considered good, average, or do over. ("Do Over" equals an "F" grade, but the grade for the revised—done over—commercial also counts.) A sample rubric for the commercial is below:

Superior:	Persuasive—includes convincing reasons, facts, information
	Understandable—clear, precise, accurate, direct
	Production—attention getting, well rehearsed, no error
	Creative—unique, original, memorable
Good:	Persuasive—has some strong, but not fully convincing reasons
	Understandable—key points were obvious but not exact
	Production—generally kept audience's attention, one or two errors
	Creative—good idea, but not unique
Average:	Persuasive—some information, but left doubts
	Understandable—audience had to figure out some meanings
	Production—some problems with organization, several errors
	Creative—relied on borrowed ideas
Do Over:	Persuasive—little information, not convincing
	Understandable—confusing, weak delivery
	Production—random, awkward, not prepared
	Creative—no new ideas, generic, and ordinary

Aphorisms

This chapter has presented step 2 of a process that can help create lessons and school cultures that increase the fascination level. This chapter also has presented a rubric that can serve as a model for qualitative assessment of student work. The foundation for this chapter was survey responses, which provided perspective on skills or knowledge that students need and perspective on how teachers could effectively teach to gain the fascination of students. Before we move to step 3 of the lesson planning, designing, and implementing process, some aphorisms can now be stated:

(1) School is boring for many students much of the time and probably for all students some of the time.

(2) Learning is fascinating.

(3) Teachers who are fascinated with learning, with students, and with causing students to learn are more likely to fascinate students with school and with learning at school than are other teachers.

(4) Teaching did not occur unless learning did occur.

(5) Fascinating teaching is not a function of the teacher's personality; rather, it is a function of the teacher's attitude, enthusiasm, work ethic, challenge to students, encouragement of students, variation of teaching methods, connecting learning with the real lives students are living now, and the broader real life that society is living now.

(6) All students can and must learn. All teachers can and must cause learning. Therefore, schools can be places where all teachers and all students are fascinated with, by, and through learning.

(7) Vibrant, energetic, intellectual, sincere interaction between teachers and students helps build fascinating classrooms and fascinating schools.

(8) Every student is fascinated with something in life; therefore, every student can be fascinated with other parts of life, including learning at school.

(9) A teacher whose teaching is not fascinating can be shown how to become a fascinating teacher.

(10) Never before has our society relied so much on education to guide lives of young people; however, never before have so many young people seen school as boring and irrelevant or as something that has to be tolerated.

The challenging reality confronting those ten aphorisms is that schools as organizations and educators as individual workers are being asked to accept more responsibilities, do more work, accomplish more with all students, complete more training, provide more services, and accommodate more diversity, special needs, and difficult societal/family situations.

The encouraging aspect of those ten aphorisms is embedded in this truth—children and teenagers are inherently fascinating and fascinated people, are inherently eager to learn, and are inherently fascinate-able by new learning, which can include learning at school. Examples of this inherent fascination are "How does that work?" "I'm old enough to do that," "Show me how to do that," "Let me see that, please," "How can I solve this problem?" "How can I get out of this mess?" "I'm interested in that job, how do I qualify for it?" "Watch me. I can do something new," and "Who is that new student? I've got to meet her/him?"

Where Fascination Already Thrives

The hope is that making school a fascinating place will have a multiplier effect. Attendance could improve at a fascinating school. Behavior could improve. The drop-out rate could change directions as more students stay through graduation. Parent, guardian, and community interest plus support could increase.

There are parts of schools where these results are already being obtained, such as athletics. Coaches can tell endless stories about students whose involvement in sports improved their attendance, their behavior, and their grades while putting them on a path to graduation. The crowds at elementary-school, middle-school, or high-school athletic events—and some other extra-curricular events such as dramatic presentations, concerts, or marching band competitions—confirm that parents, guardians, and community members will come to school for compelling reasons.

What are schools doing right with athletics? Could some of the ideas and methods of athletics also apply to other parts of schools with the result of increasing student fascination with, commitment to, and success in all parts of school?

Is there a model from which to borrow? Yes. In all of the recent efforts to reform education, there has been little or no attention given to reforming athletics in schools. We seem to be pleased with the results we are getting in athletics. Coaches are having great success getting students to work hard in sports. Our students seem to have great success with touchdowns, free throws, and homeruns. What are we doing right in sports? What could be borrowed from sports and applied to the classroom?

Coaches take their teams through practices with clearly identified purposes achieved by clearly planned activities. The list which follows provides details for a six-part sequence for practice of a school athletic team:

(1) Warm-up: stretch, light exercises, and some comments about today's practice, a recent game, or an upcoming game

(2) Drills: work on specific parts of the sport such as block, tackle, free throws

(3) Skills: apply the drill work, perhaps three football players block together or a soccer goalie and defenders work together

(4) Scrimmage: actual competition as individuals or groups match their skills

(5) Cool-down: stretch, light running

(6) Huddle: the whole team building commitment to the whole team

Coaches sometimes give out printed materials—-plays to study, rules to know, or articles to read; however, practice time is active and interactive time. Touchdowns are not merely discussed at football practice; rather, the drills and skills that can help athletes create touchdowns are practiced, applied, mastered, cheered, and rewarded.

Athletic practices are intense. Coaches speak of a successful team as having great intensity. Losing coaches often comment, "We just did not play with intensity today." What do those words—intense and intensity—mean in sports? They mean that the coaches and the players constantly (1) demand the best of themselves, (2) seek ways to improve, (3) are never settled with anything less than greatness; plus, (4) practices include every possible method and every possible challenge to develop every player's ability and potential. Players are asked to be and to become more than they realize they can be and become. In Chapter 4, the idea of intensity will be applied to classrooms and to schools.

Could that six-part sequence be borrowed by classroom teachers who seek to make their lessons as fascinating to students as sports practices or events are?

When a teacher uses the Interaction Lesson Plan steps of 1—Basic Concept and 2—Instruction Grid, could some or all of the six-part sequence used in athletics help implement and arrange specific aspects of a fascinating and "learning causing" lesson? Yes, and this six-part sequence is step 3 in our lesson-planning process.

This book presents a three-step lesson-planning and implementing process. A sample lesson using this process follows.

Step 1: Interaction Lesson Plan—Basic Concept

This lesson will cause learning:

  a. Of this idea: How the Bill of Rights impacts life in the United States.
     Of this information: The content of the Bill of Rights.
     Of this skill: Application of the Bill of Rights to real-life situations.

b. Through these activities:
   - case studies
   - simulations
   - analysis
   - recall games
   - pencil and paper drills
c. With this interaction:
   - discussion of case studies
   - each student participating in simulations
   - discussion of factual and conceptual analysis
   - each student participating in recall games
   - each student doing pencil and paper drills
d. Learning will be measured by and confirmed by this method:
   (1) The teacher will evaluate participation by each student in the discussions, simulations, and games.
   (2) The teacher will grade each student's pencil and paper work including a writing assignment and drills.

Step 2: Interaction Lesson Plan Instruction Grid

A teacher uses the grid (see Figure 3.2) for further thinking about the ideas identified in step 1 for a lesson or unit and then for identifying additional specific, detailed classroom activities and homework assignments that implement the ideas and activities listed in step 1. For example, step 1 indicated that case studies would be used. Now, a teacher reflects and mentally says, "How could case studies enhance one or more of the eight student skills and use one or more of the four teacher skills? Well, I could create some new school rules that clearly violate the Bill of Rights. This connects learning with real life at school. Students could write, maybe a letter to the editor of the school paper, about these new rules. That works on the basic skill of writing. If they read their letters in class and respond to each other in a discussion, we get communication skills put to use, plus, we stimulate thinking. OK, this is taking shape."

Note: The reader will see that the complete unit on the Bill of Rights will incorporate many of the thirty-two cells from the grid. The four cells filled in on page 50 reflect only the one lesson/activity using new school rules as the stimulus for writing, communication, and thinking.

Step 3: Interaction Lesson Plan—Six-Part Sequence

Now that a teacher has identified the basic concept in step 1 and has reflected upon and designed interaction opportunities/activities in step 2, the

	Teacher Skills			
	A **Challenge Students**	**B** **Variety of Teaching Methods**	**C** **Enthusiasm & Encourage-ment**	**D** **Connect Learning with Living**
Student Skills				
1. Basics	Write a letter to the editor			Propose new school rules
2. Communi-cation	Discuss the letters to the editor			
3. Computer Use				
4. Thinking	Respond to each other's letters			
5. Problem Solving				
6. Life-long Learning				
7. People Skills				
8. Work Ethic				

Figure 3.2.

final step is to arrange the sequence of classroom activities, homework, tests, and other instructional methods that, taken altogether, will be the implementation of the lesson or unit. The example below shows implementation of fascinating lessons that use the three-step process, including the six-part sequence, while also contrasting fascinating lessons with boring lessons. Consider the contrasting lesson plans shown below:

CONTRAST: Boring Lesson versus Fascinating Lesson
LESSON PLAN MODEL: 1—Interaction Lesson Plan—Basic Concept
                       2—Interaction Lesson Plan—Instruction
                          Grid
                       3—Six-part Sports Practice Sequence
TOPIC: The Bill of Rights

(1) Warm-up:

- *Boring Lesson:* "Today you'll complete a worksheet about the Bill of Rights. Use pages 67–72 in your book. This is really important because you will have a test on this in a few days."
- *Fascinating Lesson:* "Yesterday we read silently and then out loud the complete Bill of Rights. We also paraphrased the Bill of Rights to emphasize meaning of the original words. Now, let's put it to use.

  "From this moment on, this school has some new rules. First, the student newspaper is abolished after its next issue. Second, students may not gather in groups larger than four students. Third, no student may socialize with any student who is two grades or 2 years older or younger. Fourth, no buttons, patches, shirts, hats, or other clothing with any printed or other messages may be worn. For example, 'Save the whales' or 'God loves you' are not allowed. Fifth, any complaints about the new rules will result in the student who complained being suspended.

  "Now, write a three-paragraph letter to the editor of the school newspaper for its last issue expressing your thoughts about these new rules. Refer to the Bill of Rights at least three times in your letter. Use a pen name, just like the authors of the Federalist Papers did, to sign your letter, but include your real name at the top of the page."

(2) Drills:

- *Boring Lesson:* "First, list the rights protected in the first ten amendments. Second, match the right listed in column A with the number of the amendment to the U.S. Constitution listed in column B. Third, indicate whether the statements are true or false. Sample, statement one is 'The Bill of Rights was approved in 1776,' and that is false."
- *Fascinating Lesson:* "First, here's a list of the rights protected by the first amendment. Which of these rights apply to any of the new rules at school? Do the new rules follow the first amendment, or is there some contradiction?

  "Second, I'll mention a right. You tell me if it is protected by the Bill of Rights. If yes, which amendment? If no, should it be added? Number one, the right to own a gun. Number two, the right to drive a car. Number three, the right to a trial by jury. Number four, the right to a job.

  "Three, you've read fifty facts about the Bill of Rights. I'll give you the answer, and you give me the question. For example, the answer is '1791, not 1776 or 1789.' The correct question is 'When was the Bill of Rights added to the U.S. Constitution?' "

(3) Skills:
- *Boring Lesson:* "First, read each of the four situations on the pages I handed out. Decide if the Bill of Rights has been violated or not. Explain your answer. Second, write a fifth situation and explain how the Bill of Rights applies to the situation."
- *Fascinating Lesson:* "A teacher brings a student to the office. The teacher yells at the principal, 'This student cussed at me and threw books at me. He must be suspended now, no questions asked, he has to go now.' How could the Bill of Rights apply to this situation?

  "Try another one. The U.S. Congress decides to consider a law about guns—a citizen may own guns, but not more than three guns per citizen. Is this consistent with the second amendment or not? This law lets you own guns, but not unlimited guns."

(4) Scrimmage:
- *Boring Lesson:* "Who can answer this—what would the Constitution be like without a Bill of Rights? Any thoughts?" (Do not send the student who says "shorter" to the office for punishment. The teacher's vague, dull question caused the problem, so the teacher can solve it.)

  "Because there is no discussion about my question, half of you will write an essay saying the Constitution would still be fine and the other half will write that the Constitution would not work without the Bill of Rights."
- *Fascinating Lesson:* "The freedom to speak has limits. The U.S. Supreme Court has reasoned that you may not shout 'fire' in a crowded theater when there is no fire and your shouting could cause a deadly panic. Let's become the Supreme Court. We'll hear the evidence in a real case called *Tinker v. Des Moines.* The issue is about students wearing armbands at school to express a protest. Then, we will stage the court hearing with nine of you as justices, four of you as attorneys—two on each side—and everyone else will be news reporters covering the event. Here are the facts in the case."

(5) Cool-down:
- *Boring Lesson:* "What is the first amendment about? What is the second amendment about? What is the third amendment about? . . . and so on through all ten."
- *Fascinating Lesson:* This teacher speeds though the fifty objective facts the students have already read. Each student writes the answer, then the teacher goes through the class asking the questions sequentially to individual students and moving to the next question if the answer was right or repeating the current question until a student

is correct. This fifty-question drill takes a few minutes and can be repeated, if needed, to help all students remember all answers. The fascination increases because this activity feels like a television game show, but students are learning, attentive, and involved.

(6) Huddle:

- *Boring Lesson:* "For tomorrow, read pages 72–76, and answer the questions on page 77. Each answer is at least two complete sentences."

- *Fascinating Lesson:* "For tomorrow, be ready for a radio talk show in class. Robert and Brian will be the guests on the show. Julie will write some commercials and will play some of the real commercials we have including public service spots and some audio taped propaganda from interest groups, plus Julie will organize the callers in class—that's all of you. I'll be the host of the show. The topic is 'The government is reducing rights, not protecting rights.' Let's practice in the time left today—what is government doing to reduce or to protect rights such as trial by jury, freedom of the press, gun ownership, or freedom of religion."

Educators could benefit by trading successful ideas. Academic teachers could borrow ideas from athletic coaches. Guidance counselors at one school can borrow successful ideas from guidance counselors at other schools. Principals can get leadership and management ideas from business executives, business publications, and other principals.

The three-step process shown above is not intended to be a burden. The author can hear teachers saying, "I have too much to do now. Don't give me another idea." The reply is clear—"Because you have too much to do, you need another idea, a better idea. The three steps of the Interaction Lesson plan process can help you get better results and can help you use time more efficiently and more effectively."

Fascinating lessons can be created. Fascinating classes can be designed and implemented. Fascinating schools can be produced through the inspired, energetic, creative, determined, and enthusiastic work of educators who keep remembering why they chose teaching as a career and/or why teaching chose them as teachers—to cause learning. It is through causing learning that teachers can help enable each student to be and to become the best person he or she is capable of being and of becoming. This may take more time and effort than some teachers are accustomed to investing in lesson planning, but better lessons that cause better learning can reduce other time-consuming duties ranging from discipline problems caused by bored students to remedial instruction of failing students.

What about all the other reform efforts in education? Do we dismiss those and concentrate only on making classrooms and schools fascinating? To the extent that those reforms help teachers cause learning, the reforms are worthwhile. If a reform does not help cause learning, why does it merit any time or effort?

EDUCATION REFORM

There have been many efforts in recent years to reform education. Some of these reforms deal with the structure or organization of schools, goals for schools, finances, scheduling, or curriculum. Some of these reforms have a direct impact on the teaching that occurs in classrooms, some have an indirect impact on the teaching that occurs in classrooms, while others never get to that essential level.

Most of the time that students spend in schools is in classrooms. Most of what adults intend for students to learn in school will be delivered via the classroom. This suggests that genuine, fundamental, effective improvement of the educational experience that students have must emphasize what happens in the classroom. The Chamber of Commerce report in Chapter 1 showed that priority.

It is helpful to review some of the recent or current reform efforts in education (some details about education reform are in the appendix):

Reform	Idea of the Reform
Standards	Set higher goals, and you will get higher results.
Decentralization	Make decisions at the school level, and the decisions will have more support from people they impact.
Vouchers	Expand choice beyond the closest school to your home (or is it to get tax money to pay for private schools?).
Exit criteria	Make promotion or graduation based on results, not on time in school.
One-gender classes or schools	Isolate boys and girls to avoid bias or distractions.
Technology	Efficiency; individualized instruction; keeping current with the job market.
Special education	Help students with special needs.
Year-round scheduling	Efficiency; avoid "down-time," and increase continuity.
Block scheduling	Allows longer lessons, in-depth work.
Magnet schools	New choices, more commitment, and voluntarily diverse student bodies.

Reform	Idea of the Reform
3- and 4-year-old programs	Early childhood education is needed as a foundation for later learning.
Authentic assessment	Provide a comprehensive, realistic measure of work done rather than use the limited measure of a percentage or letter grade only.
Back to basics	Reading, writing, and arithmetic.

Those ideas can be explained in ways that would cause most reasonable people to understand them and, even if to disagree with them, at least to see why they make sense to their advocates. Here's the question—what impact would vouchers have on what a teacher teaches and on how that teacher teaches? What impact would any of the above reforms have on what is taught and on how it is taught?

Yes, some of those reforms might lead to some actions that have some impact on what some teachers do in some classrooms. It is also true that some of those reforms could be fully implemented and a boring, unproductive, ordinary teacher could continue to be boring, unproductive, and ordinary. Direct reform of ineffective teaching, rather than reform of aspects of education that surround teaching or that partially impact teaching, is the intention of the ideas in this book.

Genuine reform of boring, unproductive, ordinary teaching will require that teachers who are not causing learning because they are boring, unproductive, ordinary teachers are shown how to teach better and are required to do what better teachers do. To borrow from science, a teacher who is boring remains boring until acted on by a fascinating force. What are those fascinating forces? Here is a partial list, please add more:

- Observe fascinating teachers and start doing what they do.
- Go to some plays, musicals, and concerts, and see what captivates an audience. Then figure out how you could apply that in your classroom.
- Take an acting class—learn how to make fascinating performances, and apply that skill in your classroom.
- Read the Sunday *New York Times*—more than a local newspaper ever can, it can help make you think of thoughts and become aware of information that you would miss. Read the *Economist* for global ideas.
- Act in a local dramatic production.
- Play on a local adult recreational team—remind yourself why students love to learn how to play games and sports.
- Watch children at a park, and see how they learn, explore, and interact.

- Talk to students—ask them what would fascinate them. [Note: a word of reality and of caution—do not let students hide behind the excuse "That teacher is so boring" when you know that the teacher is offering good lessons that other students are finding fascinating. When some students use the word "boring," they may really mean "Wow, we sure do have a lot of work in that class."]
- Plan a month of lessons that do not use the textbook.
- Plan a month of lessons that use only original materials that you create—use no materials prepared by a textbook publisher or any other provider—make yourself think through the content of each task you will ask students to do rather than letting someone else do that thinking for you.
- Borrow ideas from television game shows, and use those ideas in your classrooms; this includes rewards and keeping score and being excited.
- Be sure that what you are doing in your classroom can pass the *now* test—what difference does this material make to students now? The answer has to be more than "If they don't learn it, they flunk" or "Because."
-
-
-
-
-

I Refuse; I Insist

I refuse to become one of you. I refuse to become an ordinary educator who knows only two facts—how long until summer vacation and how long until retirement.

I refuse to join the teachers' lounge gossip about students or parents or weekends. I do not come to school for the lounge. I come to school for the students. I come to school to cause learning.

I refuse to let the copy machine or the VCR teach my students.

I refuse to come in at 8 A.M. and leave at 3 P.M. and complain about how little work the students do.

I refuse to re-use last year's lesson plans. They worked with some students, but not with all students so I have to create better lesson plans.

I refuse to dress in jeans and a sweatshirt and then criticize the students or society for not respecting teachers.

I refuse to blame students, politicians, parents, laws, taxes, teacher salaries, or what students did not learn from their teachers last year for any poor work my students do. My duty is to teach the students I have—not to blame other people for my students being less than straight A, brilliant scholars and upstanding citizens.

I refuse to abandon the original dream that caused me to choose teaching and that caused teaching to choose me—the dream that I could teach any student, that I could teach every student.

I refuse to get discouraged even though I know that not every student will immediately respond to me, but many will, most will, all can. I insist on being a fascinating teacher in a fascinating classroom with students who join me in the fascinating adventure of learning. My students will be fascinated with learning because I will be fascinated with learning, with the students, and with causing the students to learn. For my students, school will be fascinating because learning will be fascinating.

I refuse to be boring or bored. I insist on being fascinating and fascinated. My students are real people living real lives. They are fascinating to me. Their education is fascinating to me. Together, we fascinate each other as we team up to cause learning, which is fascinating.

Jared and Friends

To complete the thoughts in the chapter, let's visit Jared again. His school is celebrating "Bring Your Family to School Week." The school has warmly invited parents, guardians, grandparents, uncles, aunts, and other family members of students to visit the school and to observe classes.

Jared's mother, Ms. Bethel, visited her son's Language Arts (English) class and then stayed to have lunch with Jared. They were joined by two of Jared's friends who are neighbors of the Bethels. The group sits where Jared and his friends, Owen and Heather, always sit. The three 8th graders—Jared, Owen, and Heather—have grown up together since kindergarten. Ms. Bethel felt as if she were with her own children as Owen and Heather joined the group she and Jared had started. "So, Ms. Bethel, how's school?" asked Owen.

"Yeah, Ms. B, can you do all of the work we have to do?" Heather asked with a smile.

"I think so. The vocabulary work Jared's class did was really interesting. At first I thought that vocabulary would be pretty ordinary—it was when I was in school. All we did was what the spelling book told us to do—write words, look up words, memorize words, circle answers, and take a test."

Heather put her pizza down and said, "Well, that's pretty much what our class does, right Owen?"

"Yeah, words to write and all that stuff Ms. Bethel said. That's all vocabulary ever is in our class. Is your class different, Jared?"

Jared was more interested in his pizza than in reviewing a class that was already over for the day so he just said, "Well, yeah, I guess so. We do some of what you do, but that's not all."

"I really was amazed," Ms. Bethel added. "Jared's teacher seems to use lots of different activities. In just one class period, the students used vocabulary flash cards, a vocabulary crossword puzzle, played a game—kind of like a television game show—about the vocabulary words, practiced spelling, and something else. What was it, Jared?"

"Uh," Jared's pizza still was more interesting to him, but he managed to remember, "It was pictures—those slides."

"Oh, yes. Jared's teacher had a slide that showed a picture that related to each word." Ms. Bethel seemed very excited about it all. "Heather, does your class ever do things like Jared's class did?"

"No, we never do, Ms. Bethel. We don't really care so much. We do what the teacher tells us to. It's really easy. We make good grades and move on to new words next week," Heather explained as Owen nodded his agreement.

"It's no big deal, Ms. Bethel," Owen said. "The class is boring, but it's easy. Nobody much cares."

Lunch was good this day because pizza and teenagers get along. Ms. Bethel, Jared, Owen, and Heather discussed an upcoming school play and the trip the band will take to some elementary schools. They also talked about a new student who walked by. The rumor is that the new student, Jil, likes Jared, but Jared acted as if he was not interested. Ms. Bethel was too cool to tell Owen and Heather that Jared had a phone call from Jil last night.

The signal for lunch to end is when teachers return to the cafeteria. Students line up with their teachers.

"Bye, Mom, thanks for coming. I gotta go line up with Ms. Hunter."

"OK, Jared. See you when I get home from work. Dad will be late, so you and I can fix supper."

"Mom, can we order pizza, please?"

Before Ms. Bethel could answer, Ms. Hunter walked up. "Ms. Bethel, it was so good to have you in class. Thanks for being here."

"Ms. Hunter, that was a wonderful class. Everyone was on the edge of their seats, paying attention, learning. I was impressed."

"Well, most people at our school are convinced that these students can learn anything and everything. They are bright and energetic. We try to put their curiosity and their energy to good use, even with vocabulary lessons. Right, Jared."

"Yes. That's right. Uh, Ms. Hunter, don't you think my Mom and I should give ourselves a bonus and have pizza for supper tonight?" Jared emphasized the word *bonus*.

Ms. Hunter and Ms. Bethel had to smile. "A bonus, huh?"

"Yeah, Mom, bonus is one of this week's vocabulary words, right? See what I learned!"

"OK, Jared, pizza it is. Now, go do some bonus learning in your next class."

"OK, Mom. Thanks."

Making Vocabulary Fascinating

What had Ms. Hunter done in vocabulary class today? She had fascinated her students with parts of the vocabulary week process she used. From Friday through Friday, this sequence was followed by Ms. Hunter to cause her students to learn vocabulary words and much more.

(1) On Friday, the students in Ms. Hunter's language arts class are given a list of ten words. She has written the words on the board before class. Each student copies the words. It is expected that each student will complete this with no instruction or reminder. Some students arrive early to do this, and others get it done during class.

The words this week were agriculture, bonus, century, donate, education, fraternity, habitat, invent, freedom, and sorority. All of these words have a Latin language origin, and Ms. Hunter will use that in her lessons. Several of these words relate to other classes the students take—science and social studies especially—and Ms. Hunter will reward students when they make an interdisciplinary connection in class discussion or on written work. The science and social studies teachers were given the list so they can use these words intentionally and acknowledge students who use these words.

(2) By Monday, each student will have made a set of ten flash cards, one card per word. The word is on one side. The definition and a picture that represents the word are on the other side. Ms. Hunter grades these and returns them Tuesday. She does not just superficially check in class to see if the cards were done or not. She takes them home and reads them. She writes a response to each student. If homework is to be taken seriously by her students, Ms. Hunter knows that the students must see her take their effort seriously.

(3) The students will work in pairs to create a crossword puzzle that uses the ten words. Some are put on the board for the class to solve. The whole class worked a puzzle Ms. Hunter made that used the ten words and their Latin language origins.

(4) Ms. Hunter will lead the students in vocabulary "Jeopardy," which is similar to the television game show. Ms. Hunter gives the definition, and students respond. For example, the clue "100 years" is followed by "What is a century?" Ms. Hunter includes words from previous weeks to build the students' memory of those former words.

(5) "The 4-Minute Drill"—Ms. Hunter gives the meaning, and students cite the word, or Ms. Hunter gives the word, and the student spells that word. Ms. Hunter moves quickly from student to student to see how many correct replies can be obtained in 4 minutes using only the ten words for this week. There is some value in some repetition, plus the students try to beat their class score from the 4-minute drill last week. "May we do that again, please" is often heard after a 4-minute drill.

(6) Each student individually writes a letter using the ten words correctly. The letter has to make sense, use complete sentences, and be given to an adult at school or at home. Students do not write to the same adult 2 weeks in a row. The adult, in agreement with Ms. Hunter, checks the accuracy of the letter and responds, in writing, to the student. The students' letters and the responses are returned to Ms. Hunter the next day for her review, for a grade to be assigned, and for the students to get their letter and the reply.

(7) Pictures—Ms. Hunter shows slides, CD-ROM pictures, posters, or photographs to illustrate each of the ten words. Students explain the association between the word and the picture, but first have to spell the word they think is best represented by the picture. As a variation, Ms. Hunter will sometimes play a CD or a tape of a song that represents a word.

(8) Practice Quiz—this usually happens on Thursday, but Wednesday is fine depending on the time that was needed to complete items 2 through 7. Ms. Hunter says each word. Each student writes the word, defines the word, and writes a sentence using the word. These are graded in class by Ms. Hunter and the students.

(9) The Test—This is Thursday or Friday, 1 day after the practice quiz. A grade of 80% is required. Bonus points this week came from answering questions about the Latin origins of the words. Students who score 80% or higher do enrichment work. The students who scored less than 80% are retaught the ten words with direct instruction by Ms. Hunter, pencil and paper work, drill and practice, an 8-minute drill, which is a long 4-minute drill, and/or some unique methods depending on who the students are in this group and what works best with them according to Ms. Hunter's insight.

Ms. Hunter's students are given many responsibilities in the vocabulary learning process. Ms. Hunter challenges the students to acquire information about the words, to apply that information, to repeatedly, yet in varying ways, put the information into meaningful experiences, and to study the words. The classroom pace is vibrant, even aggressive. The variety of activities addresses realities about attention spans and learning styles. Ms. Hunter paces the class and leads class with an intentional intensity, but not with chaos or stress. Ms. Hunter is in charge. Lessons are planned. Progress will be made with some scheduling flexibility available, if needed, such as "Let's do one more 4-minute drill to be sure we all know this."

Ms. Hunter knows that children and teenagers can move at a bold pace in their learning, but that without the teacher creating the intensity, many students will move at the slowest acceptable pace. Intensity supports fascination. Intellectual intensity and instructional intensity are not obtained simply by teaching rapidly; rather, intellectual intensity and instructional intensity are obtained by teaching interactively, aggressively, purposefully, meaningfully, and energetically with variety and with drama to constantly inform, amaze, exercise, apply, and challenge the mind of each student.

What did the class that Owen and Heather are in do to study vocabulary?

(1) A worksheet: match the words and their definitions.

(2) Write each word ten times.

(3) Use each word in two different sentences.

(4) Complete pages 46–50 in the spelling/vocabulary book on these ten words.

(5) Study silently in class on your own.

(6) Take a test on the words.

Owen, Heather, and most students in that class were bored; however, they did not ask their teacher to do what Ms. Hunter did with her class. They lived by the unspoken agreement made in far too many classrooms—if the students behave and don't complain, they will not be asked to do much. The result is an orderly, functional, boring class in which material is covered, grades are given, no questions are asked, and the teacher gets paid. The principal of any school where "agreement classrooms" exist may accept the "agreement" because there are other emergencies that must be dealt with immediately. A boring, lifeless, uninspired classroom is also an emergency; however, that emergency arouses no alarm bell, no irate parent, no investigation, no taxpayer complaint, and no action. That is unacceptable.

Fascinating lessons, fascinating classrooms, and fascinating schools that captivate students, that simultaneously challenge and fulfill teachers, and that cause learning are possible; therefore, the boring lesson, the boring classroom, and the boring school are unacceptable. Chapter 4 will go into further detail about how fascinating learning experiences are created. First, some words of guidance from an 8th grader I taught and words of reality about what it is like to be a child or teenager today.

PARENTS AND TEACHERS

Parents are too forceful. Parents think that whatever they say goes. Well, I think that they are wrong to think that. Some parents don't think their children have a brain or feelings or common sense. Parents are always complaining about not getting any respect, and yet they turn around and have not one grain of respect when it comes to young people. In my hometown, my church's youth group made a list for parents to take a look-see and try some of these rules:

(1) Don't give me everything I ask for. Sometimes I am just testing you to see how much I can get.

(2) Don't always be giving orders. If you suggest something instead of giving a command, I will do it faster.

(3) Don't compare me with anybody else, especially a brother or a sister. If you make me out to be smarter or better, somebody gets hurt, and if you make me out to be dumber or worse, then I get hurt.

(4) Let me do as much for myself as I can. That's how I learn. If you do everything for me, I will never be able to do anything for myself.

(5) Don't correct my mistakes in front of other people. Tell me how to improve when nobody is around.

(6) Don't scream at me. It makes me scream back, and I don't want to be a screamer.

(7) When I do something wrong, don't try to get me to tell you why I did it. Sometimes I don't know why.

Now, about teachers. I've learned to get to know how my teachers operate the first week of school. So, I think my advice to teachers will help. Some complaints of mine might refer to you if you're a teacher.

(1) Sometimes being a teacher is like being a parent. So, please, don't compare me with anybody else, don't correct me in front of others, and don't try to pry the excuses out of me when I don't know why I did something wrong.

(2) If you always give me orders, I will turn rebellious. If you compare me with somebody else, somebody will get hurt. If you correct my mistakes in front of others, I get embarrassed and angry. If you try to pry the excuses from me when I don't even know, I might end up lying and getting into bigger trouble.

(3) Try to make your class more interesting and exciting. My history teacher has a very exciting and interesting class. He rewards my classmates and me when we play trivia and even encourages us for just trying to answer a question. He also has a sense of humor, which every teacher needs. He always asks you to do something for him or for yourself. He never orders.

(4) One of my favorite reasons for him being a good teacher is that he can relate to teenagers. It's always easy to talk about your problems with him

because he understands you and your problems. He often helps you work them out.

(5) He also makes the day more enjoyable when we have a test and he slips in something that has not the slightest thing to do with the subject, but it is something we can all answer. His class is fun and academic, which is on a scale of one to ten, about a twelve.

The student's insight into school is revealing. Some insight into students follows.

GROWING UP

I am more difficult, more demanding, and more threatening than ever. I also am more fascinating and more vibrant than ever.

I have been studied and explored, researched and task forced. I am the topic of workshops, special panels, scientific studies, and college courses. I am still outside of your understanding.

I take many victims with me. Some people endure and get along. Others are scarred for life. I make no deals, and I offer little sympathy. Most people are on their own when they confront me, but they can find help if they seek it.

I can be exciting, productive, and good. Too often, people expect me to be painful, rugged, and rough. I need not be a series of one trial followed by one error endlessly. I can be a path with a clear goal and with a right direction.

I am something that all people have in common, but I am different for every person. I am not talked about much with honesty, but people just assume that I will happen the way I should.

My current reputation is not very good. Professional experts say that I am life threatening to many people. I may have been difficult in earlier times, but it bothers me that people say I am associated with suicide or depression. I like me, and I would hope that other people could like their association with me.

I am a book with many pages, but all of them are blank. You get to write your own story.

I am a stage with no actors or props. You get to create the show.

I am growing up. You know, like, I mean, well, um, the process of making sense out of life and out of yourself.

I am the ages between childhood and adult, between being totally cared for and being totally caring toward other people. I am the crucial transition period when so much can go wrong, like pimples the day of a date or an F on a test.

I am the time when life should be lovely and hope should be unlimited. Too often, growing up is a battle. I hope it will be a bold adventure for you.

I am growing up, and I seek to be everything you need me to be so you will be everything you should be and can be and are meant to be.

Author's note: My student stated that our history class was fun. It was not designed to be fun or to be unfun. It was designed to be fascinating, energetic, intellectual, interactive, demanding, and rewarding. Fun was a by-product, a very lovely by-product. If a class is fascinating, intellectually challenging, and really captures the students' interest, they will say that it was "fun." They are not going to say, except humorously, "Our class was a very intellectual experience that caused me to learn while applying higher order thinking skills."

CHAPTER 4

Creating Fascinating Learning Experiences

How? Much that is presented to teachers by principals, superintendents, school boards, or training sessions deals with (A) *what* has to be accomplished—safer schools, reducing failure rates, involving parents or guardians more or (B) *why* change is needed—a new law, a new policy, an angry community group, a research study, or a media story. There is less provided about *how.*

This book is built on several premises: (1) every student can learn, (2) every student must learn, (3) every school can cause every student to learn, and (4) every teacher can and must cause every one of his or her students to learn. This book also is built upon two realities: (1) school is boring, and (2) learning is fascinating. This chapter emphasizes actions that teachers can implement to make classes, classrooms, and schools fascinating places where students and teachers team up to cause learning.

This chapter is devoted to *how.*

INTELLECTUAL INTENSITY
AND INSTRUCTIONAL INTENSITY

INTELLECTUAL intensity and instructional intensity are not obtained simply by teaching rapidly; rather, by teaching interactively, aggressively, purposefully, meaningfully, energetically with a variety, and with drama to constantly inform, amaze, exercise, apply, and challenge the mind of each student so learning is caused.

Henry David Thoreau wisely commented in *Walden:* "There is more to life than increasing its speed." For teachers, there is more to creating a fascinating classroom than increasing the speed with which boring tasks are assigned to bored students. "Do more worksheets—faster, faster" will not create fascinated students or fascinating teaching. Doing more boring things will not create fascination. Doing boring things at a faster pace will not create fascination.

Doing purposeful and meaningful things, in ways that are vibrant, dramatic, varied, energetic, meaningful, and challenging in a classroom where the teacher and the students continually interact can cause fascinated students and fascinating teaching. It is this teaching, composed of instructional intensity, coupled with intellectual intensity, that can inspire the genuine, compelling, irresistible interaction between teacher and students that can create fascinating classrooms and fascinating schools in which learning is caused.

Intellectual intensity is not satisfied with "yes" or "no" questions and answers, although some of those questions are needed; rather, intellectual intensity probes, explores, imagines, analyzes, explains, reasons, and understands. Sure, some facts and skills must be mastered, but even that objective data or procedural aspect of the learning process (1) can be vibrant and meaningful and (2) can be the basis for dynamic, intense intellectual exercise that puts facts and skills to use as minds and ideas interact.

Instructional intensity is not satisfied with "covering material," handing out another set of publisher-produced worksheets, or sitting at a desk while students passively and thoughtlessly write mundane answers to banal questions from the end of a meaningless chapter in a boring textbook. Instructional intensity is seen in a classroom where a teacher who is fascinated with learning and who is fascinated with students convinces the students to join in today's compelling adventure of thinking, discovering, creating, reasoning, acquiring, correcting, questioning, memorizing, reading, discussing, writing, calculating, and knowing. This above average method of teaching—the method of intellectual intensity and of instructional intensity—can help invigorate a teacher, a student, a classroom, and a school and can help people transcend a life of averageness.

THE AVERAGE PERSON LIVES . . .

70 average years, or

840 average months, or

3,640 average weeks, or

25,550 average days, or

613, 200 average hours, or 36,792,000 average minutes.

BUT—maybe there is this 1 minute,

when you get this one idea,

and you think about it for 1 hour,

and you talk about it for 1 day,

and you research it for 1 week,

and you plan it for 1 month,

and you live it for 1 year,

and you are not average any more.

School districts pay full salaries to many teachers who are average. School districts pay full salaries to many teachers who are below average or who are above average. The pay scale is often a function of how many years of experience an educator has combined with how much college/graduate education that educator has. That system will change slowly, if ever. That is not the issue. The issue is why be average when greatness is within reach? Why be boring and bored when fascination is possible?

This chapter will deeply explore the "how" of creating fascinating classrooms and fascinating schools—those places known for their instructional intensity and intellectual intensity. The emphasis in this chapter is implementation.

Implementing Fascinating Lessons

What does Mr. Prather know that Ms. Armstrong does not know? What does Ms. Hunter know that her boring colleague does not know? Are their beliefs, attitudes, and convictions different? Are they all devoted to causing learning for all students? If some teachers are not so devoted to students, could the administration of a school at least require changes in instruction so teachers use the activities, pace, and methods that are associated with fascination?

For all students to learn, much has to change in education, in families, and in society because all students have not been learning. For all teachers to teach at high levels of effectiveness, much has to change in how teachers teach, how teachers are trained in college and beyond, and in how teachers are evaluated. The emphasis in this chapter is on how teachers teach so that it is done in a more fascinating way, which causes learning more effectively.

We will follow part of the six-part sequence from page 48, so first the brain needs to be warmed-up. Please reflect on the following thoughts, and then write a response to each thought.

Warm-Up

(1) If and when the adults—teachers, administrators, parents, guardians— do what they tell the students to do to succeed at school, the results will surpass many current goals for education.
Response:

(2) Materials created by a conscientious teacher are usually better than materials that come with a textbook.
Response:

(3) Be the teacher you wish all of your teachers had been, and you may get the good results from students you have always wished would occur.
Response:

(4) Why do we take society's most energetic and curious members—children and teenagers aged 5 through 18—and tell them to sit down and listen for 13 years?
Response:

(5) Do school as a teacher the way you expect students to do school as students.
Response:

(6) Teach every minute of every class on every school day of the year. This includes Mondays, Fridays, the days before or after a vacation, the first day of the school year, and the last day of the school year.
Response:

(7) To convince students to be fascinated with school, show them that you are fascinated with school, with learning, and with students.
Response:

(8) Think outside of the box—for 1 month, set aside the textbook, use only teacher prepared materials, turn off the copy machine, borrow the best ideas from your most capable teaching colleagues, and teach the way the best teachers you ever had taught.
Response:

(9) When a student misbehaves and blames another student for provoking the misbehavior, say, "If she does what is wrong, you can still do what is right."
Response:

(10) Put up the following poster in your classroom: "Amaze adults—obey. Don't see what you can get away with, see what you can do away with—like getting in trouble, being checked-on all the time, and being doubted."
Response:

Drill

Good, now the brains are warmed-up so it is drill time, which is used for work on specific aspects of our endeavor. For example, if the textbook is not going to be relied on to provide the schedule, the structure, the pace, the content, and the homework for a class, what other materials or resources can be used in addition to the textbook? Textbooks can still be used in fascinating classrooms, but many, many more materials or resources need to be used also. Be honest—how many students have ever said "That textbook changed my life"? The following are *materials/resources to be used in a fascinating classroom* (space at the end is for ideas from the reader):

(1) Historical documents

(2) Discussion in class

(3) Guest speakers

(4) Photographs or slides

(5) Audiotapes

(6) Videotapes: *Warning*—Audiotapes and videotapes cannot merely be played and watched/heard. The teacher and the students must discuss, analyze, and react to the video or audio. The teacher must pre-listen to or preview tapes.

(7) Skits

(8) The Internet

(9) Local citizens, business people, political leaders as guest speakers

(10) Pen pals

(11) Newspapers—local, national, and international

(12) News magazines—national and international

(13) Documentary films/television programs

(14) Experiments, labs, or other demonstrations

(15) Artwork or music

(16) Ideas students write about

(17) Library books

(18) Computer software

(19) CD-ROM material

(20) Interviews conducted by students

(21) Other teachers

(22) Parents, guardians, grandparents, other relatives

(23) The superintendent of schools or other district level administrators

(24) Classified employees, such as the cafeteria manager, to discuss restaurant management careers

(25) University or college professor and students, including their work, such as dissertations

(26) Retired teachers

(27) Research conducted by students

(28) Field trips

(29) Textbooks from other countries—what would a British history textbook from England tell us about events of 1776?

(30) Foreign exchange students

(31) Activities in which students work in groups

(32)

(33)

(34)

(35)

(36)

Skills

Having warmed-up and completed the drill work, the next part in the sequence is skills. In this part, the drill work is applied. For example, select four of the materials/resources on the above list and explain how a fascinating lesson could be created using those materials. To do this, the Interaction Lesson Plan—Basic Concept will be used:

The purpose of this lesson is to cause learning:

(a) Of this idea: _____

(b) Through this experience: _____

(c) With this interaction: _____

(d) Learning will be measured and confirmed by this method: _____

OK, let's go through an example of this part together, and then the reader can try this part on your own.

The purpose of this lesson is to cause learning:

(a) Of this idea: Negative peer pressure can be resisted.

(b) Through this experience: (1) The teacher and students discuss the ideas of negative and positive peer pressure. (2) Students will divide into groups of four. (3) All students will watch four different 1-minute videos that portray typical situations when negative peer pressure is used: to steal from a store, to cheat on a test, to drink alcohol, and to sexually harass someone.

(c) With this interaction: (1) Each student will write his or her ideas on how to resist the peer pressure. Each group will hear the ideas from each member and then agree on one action, which will be presented as a skit to the class. (2) The teacher, a school counselor, and the students discuss/analyze each skit to determine the best ways to resist negative peer pressure.

(d) Learning will be measured and confirmed by: (1) the involvement of each student in the discussion/analysis of each skit and (2) completion of a short writing assignment: the best ways to resist negative peer pressure.

Now, turn to Figure 3.1 on page 43 and check the Basic Concept in terms of the Instruction Grid. Is there enough interaction between students, the teacher, and ideas? How many of the eight student skills will be used and improved in this lesson? How many teacher skills will be used and improved in this lesson? If necessary, make changes in the Basic Concept as guided by the Instruction Grid.

Your turn to create a lesson. Select the idea, the experience, the interaction, and the measuring. Use four ideas from the list of non-textbook materials/resources. You may use the textbook, but you must also use four other materials/resources.

The purpose of this lesson is to cause learning:

(a) Of this idea:

(b) Through this experience:

(c) With this interaction:

(d) Learning will be measured and confirmed by:

Summary

Notice, please, that the lesson about negative peer pressure included part 4, scrimmage—when individuals and groups thought of ways to resist negative peer pressure and then all groups made presentations to the total class, and part 5, cool-down—as the teacher, school counselor, and students discussed/analyzed the ideas they had seen/heard in class. The lesson prepared by the reader may have included those steps, or those steps can be added as what the teacher and students will do the next day. Some topics require days or weeks to learn, and the six-part sequence does not have to squeeze into one day or into one class period.

In the peer pressure lesson, part 6, huddle, could come the next day as the teacher and the students identify specific actions to take right then, right there in their classroom, and at their school to resist and to reduce negative peer pressure.

The Interactive Lesson Plan—Basic Concept and the six-part sequence, which is borrowed from athletic team practices, combine to provide a process that can help create fascinating lessons; however, it is necessary to include instructional intensity and intellectual intensity or the process could be ordinary instead of fascinating. To check for instructional and intellectual intensity, the peer pressure lesson needs to pass the test of the thirty-two-cell grid on page 43. Of course, the lesson is not expected to include all thirty-two cells, but intensity can be created if several or many of those cells are at work in a classroom at the same time or in a very certain sequence.

Our process for creating fascinating lessons has three steps:

(1) The Interaction Lesson Plan—Basic Concept
(2) The Interaction Lesson Plan—Instruction Grid
(3) The Six-Part Sequence

Were the students challenged in the lesson/activities about peer pressure? Yes, they did not passively watch a 30-minute "Just Say No" video or read a chapter about peer pressure and write answers to questions with no response from the teacher. They did hear from the teacher at the start of class as they discussed peer pressure. They watched 4 minutes of videos. They wrote individual responses to each video. They created group responses to each video and performed a skit. They interacted with their teacher, school counselor, and each other in a discussion/analysis. The classroom was active and interactive.

Did the teacher use a variety of teaching methods? Yes, with particular emphasis on methods that provoked communication, thinking, problem-solving, and people skills.

Was there enthusiasm and encouragement? The opportunities were certainly present. If the teacher moved throughout the room and interacted with each group, there could be much encouragement as skits were created.

Did the learning connect with living? Yes, peer pressure is real and is not limited to children or teenagers. Adults pressure each other. The learning could apply to the current life of the students and to their later years.

Was there any work on the basics—reading, writing, and mathematics? Yes, students wrote a response to their video, and there was a concluding writing assignment.

Were computers used? No, and despite the current technology obsession in education, it is acceptable to teach a lesson without a computer; however, it is not acceptable to resist computer use.

Did the lesson apply to life-long learning? It certainly can if the teacher shows an example of adults using peer pressure on each other. The students could probably cite times they have seen adults use peer pressure or could present a skit showing adults reacting to peer pressure. The teacher and counselor could be in that skit.

How did the lesson relate to work ethic? The teacher exemplified a commendable work ethic by preparing a multi-dimensional lesson, rather than merely worksheeting the students. The students were given many tasks and duties so the work ethic expected of them was substantial.

The peer pressure lesson passed the Instruction Grid reality check because the lesson was designed using the grid! Now, please check the lesson you designed on pages 71–72 against the Instructional Grid to add specific, detailed activities that will create intellectual intensity and instructional intensity. As you do that, think also of the six-part sequence so you can begin to arrange and schedule the exact flow of this lesson or unit.

The Student Perspective

What would Jared have to say about the peer pressure lesson? He and his friends will give their thoughts below. Jared, Heather, and Owen do have some elective classes together including health class where they all were involved in the lesson on peer pressure. This conversation was at their lunch table:

Jared: You had to get all the attention in that skit, didn't you? Do you see a movie career in your future, Heather?

Heather: Maybe I can get you a role in my first movie, Jared.

Owen: You are such a brown-noser, Heather. You just kissed up to the teacher. That class is dumb. We always have to do silly things. I hate that class.

Heather: You hate work. That class makes you do something instead of sit and goof off. All you do at home is watch TV so you should have liked the videos we watched. That class is better than others where you just listen or watch and never do anything.

Owen: You just like to perform for an audience. You'll be Homecoming Queen someday, and this is your practice time for the beauty pageant. Maybe you'll be Miss America.

Jared: Back off you guys. That class was OK. We have classes that are a lot worse, you know, dull lectures or dumb textbooks. I was just teasing Heather about her performance. She's an actress, but she also makes good grades. What's wrong with getting to act in class. Those skits were kind of cool.

Heather: Anyone could make good grades. It's not that tough. I'd rather do skits than dumb ditto sheets.

Owen: I guess you're talking about me. OK, I make bad grades, and I'd rather have simple classes where we don't do much. My parents get on me about it. Teachers always say I don't work up to my ability. They say I don't turn in work and I daydream. So what. School is boring. I am going to be a musician, anyway. I don't need school. I just need my guitar.

Jared: That's true, you play guitar great. Are you still trying to start a band?

Owen: Yeah. We're getting together to practice after school almost every day. It's cool. We know a few songs, and we sound OK. We might play at the next school dance.

Heather: OK, you'll be a musician, and I'll be an actress. I'm in a show next month. It's a musical, and I get to sing a solo. If you come see me, I'll give you an autograph.

Jared: Yeah, right. If you come to my karate class, I'll kick a board in half and sign the pieces for you. Come today and you can watch me test for my next belt.

Heather: Jared, dear, I must go to the theater today to rehearse for my debut. I will think of you while we are apart.

Jared: Jared, dear? Come on, Heather. People will think something is going on between us.

Heather: You had your chance, Jared. You'll be sorry when I'm famous. Anyway. I do have rehearsal today after school. Maybe Owen can watch you at karate.

Owen: No way. My band has a serious practice today. Kick boards, Jared. Break a leg, Heather. I gotta go.

Jared: See ya, Owen. Hey, Heather.

Heather: Not now, Jared, dear. I must go. Class starts in a few minutes. Maybe I'll get to perform again. Some teachers do recognize my talent.

Jared: Yeah and some teachers just let you act to pass the time. See ya, Heather.

Heather: Parting is such sweet sorrow; except when I'm leaving you, Jared.

Are Jared, Heather, and Owen fascinated about karate, acting, and guitar, respectively? Yes. What makes karate, acting, and playing guitar so fascinating to these 14-year-olds? Is there anything from karate, acting, or playing guitar that a teacher could apply in the classroom to make Jared, Heather, and Owen equally fascinated with reading, writing, arithmetic, and other work at school?

Yes. Karate is three-dimensional. Acting is three-dimensional. Playing guitar is three-dimensional.

Three-Dimensional Learning

Three-dimensional means that the learning is caused via (1) a variety of purposefully planned activities (2) that are meaningful, energetic, and dramatic (3) that use interaction to reach a depth of thinking that informs, amazes, exercises, applies, and challenges the mind of each student.

Jared's karate class provides a good example of three-dimensional teaching and learning. Heather's acting or Owen's guitar playing also exemplify three-dimensional work. This chapter is highly interactive, so Jared's example is shown in Figure 4.1. The reader will then complete the charts about Heather and Owen.

Worksheets? Chapter to read? Questions to answer in complete sentences? Those could be part of effective karate instruction, but what parent would be satisfied if his or her child continued going to karate class for weeks and did nothing but filled out multiple-choice questions on lifeless worksheets?

"Yeah, but karate is physical. It's easy to get students interested in kicking each other. When you teach in the typical classroom and have the usual curriculum, most of what is available is books or papers or things like that."

The education skeptics whose traditional perspective is cited in the above paragraph could be descendants of people who favored the horse and buggy over the car. Of course, books and papers are used in school. Much learning can be caused by using books and paper, but books and paper are not the only resources that can cause learning in a classroom. Rather than rejecting the

Dimension	Karate
1ST DIMENSION: A variety of purposefully planned activities.	• The importance, the need for, and the use of the activities is convincingly explained. • The skills that must be mastered for each level are precisely identified. • Instruction, drills, and practice that relate to each skill are explained and demonstrated and any questions are answered.
2ND DIMENSION: The activities are meaningful, energetic, and dramatic.	• Students work individually, in pairs, or in groups. • The action and interaction of drills and demonstrations are dramatic in mental demands and in physical results. • The connection between drills, skills, and reaching a valuable goal (the next karate belt) are clear. • The instructor participates with students, showing by example the required energy and obtainable benefits of the activities.
3RD DIMENSION: Use interaction to inform, amaze, exercise, apply, and challenge the mind of each student.	• The instructor challenges each student to think first, practice second, and demonstrate third; the instructor exemplifies the desired results. • Students and instructors interact according to tradition and need; students interact/drill with each other; many opportunities exist for total group and small group interaction. • Activities are analyzed so students master the "how" of doing karate and the "why" of doing karate in the required way.

Figure 4.1.   *Jared's Karate Class.*

karate example because "Well, I'd never let my students get up in the classroom and kick each other," try thinking outside of the box that holds all the teaching methods that are typically used.

Ask yourself "What is there about a karate class that so fascinates students that I could borrow from karate and apply in my classroom?" Go watch karate classes. Talk to karate instructors and karate students. You could learn from each other!

Heather really likes acting. As a 14-year-old 8th grader, she has high hopes of acting in high-school plays. She dreams of the auditions, the rehearsals, and of the performances. She knows some older teenagers who have made money by acting in local television commercials. She is fascinated by the possibilities that acting holds for her.

Complete the chart shown in Figure 4.2, similar to the chart about Jared's karate class. It is not necessary to be an acting class expert, just complete the chart with ideas that capture the purpose, the energy, and the interaction that an acting class can offer. For help, the chart is started.

Owen is not very excited about school, but Owen does get excited about playing guitar. He loves to play guitar alone, and he especially likes to "jam"

Dimension	Acting
1ST DIMENSION: A variety of purposefully planned activities.	● The goals, tasks, and importance of today's class are clearly explained at the start. ● The continuity between past classes, today's class, and future classes/performances is emphasized. ● The presentation of each activity is compelling, thorough, and inspiring. ● ● ●
2ND DIMENSION: The activities are meaningful, energetic, and dramatic.	● The students simultaneously see, hear, think, and do acting. ● Participation in the activities shows each student that he or she is (A) experiencing the purpose of the class—"Hey, I'm learning" or (B) needs to experience the purpose—"This is tough. Help me." ● ● ●
3RD DIMENSION: Use interaction to inform, amaze, exercise, apply, and challenge the mind of each student.	● The instructor interacts with individuals, pairs, or groups. ● The instructor leads students to be more, to do more, to probe deeper, to be intense, to be gentle—to not accept the first attempt as the only option or as the best result. ● The instructor asks questions, participates, demonstrates, and encourages. ● ● ●

Figure 4.2. Heather's Acting Class.

with friends who play other instruments. Having a successful band is Owen's dream, similar to Heather's hopes about plays and commercials.

There is much at school that teachers could do to show Owen that school relates to music. Does Owen realize the importance of mathematics in the way musical sounds, notes, octaves, and harmonies occur? Does he realize that the study of words, language, short stories, or poetry could apply to writing lyrics? Is he in the band or music class at school? Could his science project relate to music? Could he research the importance of music by various ethnic groups throughout American history rather than writing one more report about one more otherwise forgotten person from 1873? All of these options are possible. Owen's interest in music could be applied by aware teachers as a way to build some school commitment from Owen and fascination about learning at school in Owen.

Now, what can teachers learn from the commitment Owen has made to playing guitar and to the fascination he has with having a successful band? First, realize that Owen does make commitments and that Owen does have fascinations. He is not aimless or apathetic, despite what adults at school may conclude. Second, he is not very interested in school, but that could change if school could borrow some elements from Owen's guitar playing and from Owen's band.

Note: Owen's example (Figure 4.3) is different from Jared's karate class or Heather's acting class because when Owen plays his guitar by himself, he is the student and the teacher. He creates the lesson, the activities, the energy, and the interaction. When his band members practice together, they are students and teachers. Think of what happens in these settings of a 14-year-old musician alone or of teenaged band members. What causes them to work, to practice, to endure, to learn, and to become fascinated?

Why is Jared fascinated with karate?

Why is Heather fascinated with acting?

Why is Owen fascinated with guitar?

Please list reasons below, and then consider how a classroom could apply the reason (a few thought starters are provided).

Reason for Fascination	Application at School
(1) Emphasis on doing	(1) Make a model of the solar system instead of just looking at a picture in a book.
(2) Purpose was clear	(2) Connect all classroom activities to a meaningful, current benefit to students.

Dimension	Guitar; Band
1ST DIMENSION: A variety of purposefully planned activities.	• What is Owen doing? Why? • • • • What is Owen's band doing? Why? • • •
2ND DIMENSION: The activities are meaningful, energetic, and dramatic.	• What is meaningful to Owen about playing guitar? Why is playing guitar meaningful? What happens that causes Owen to commit energy to this? • • • • What causes the drama when the band plays together? • • • Why do the band members see their rehearsal as meaningful (they may call it "fun" or "cool," but it means enough to them to work at it seriously)? • •
3RD DIMENSION: Use interaction to inform, amaze, exercise, apply, and challenge the mind of each student.	• How and why is Owen's interaction with the music, the guitar, and himself challenging his mind? • • • • How and why is the band's interaction with the music, the instruments, and each other challenging their minds? • • •

Figure 4.3. Owen's Guitar Playing and Band.

Reason for Fascination	*Application at School*
(3)	*(3)*
(4)	*(4)*
(5)	*(5)*
(6)	*(6)*
(7)	*(7)*
(8)	*(8)*
(9)	*(9)*
(10)	*(10)*

Now, the many ideas presented thus far in this book can be efficiently organized to match the structure of three dimensions. The premise is that three-dimensional learning is fascinating; however, for too many students in too many classrooms, the learning is merely (1) one-dimensional—it has length, meaning it covers time from the start of class to the end of class or (2) two-dimensional—it is flat, meaning it covers a length of time and it has some width—some range of activities—but there is no depth. Three-dimensional teaching is unique for its compelling depth of instructional intensity, and intellectual intensity, which result from a variety of purposefully planned activities that have meaning, energy, and drama that are used with interaction to inform, amaze, exercise, apply, and challenge the mind of each student (see Figure 4.4).

Step 1, the Interaction Lesson Plan—Basic Concept, enables a teacher to initially think of the outline of a lesson or series of lessons. Part of that outline will be to briefly identify purposeful instructional activities to begin planning these activities. That creates the first dimension of three-dimensional teaching and learning.

Step 2, the Interaction Lesson Plan—Instruction Grid, enables a teacher to more fully develop and design the lesson or series of lessons. As the teacher

Figure 4.4. *Three-Dimensional Teaching and Learning.*

seeks ways to include the eight student skills and the four teacher methods from the grid, dimensions 2 and 3 can be created.

Step 3, the six-part sequence, enables the teacher to arrange and schedule the activities of the lesson(s) to follow an efficient, logical, and productive order so the three dimensions occur in an effective order.

Creating Three-Dimensional Teaching

1ST DIMENSION:
A variety of purpose-fully planned activities.

How to organize:
Use the Interaction Lesson Plan—Basic Concept:

1. The purpose of this lesson is to cause learning:
   a. Of this idea: _____
   _____
   _____

   b. Through these activities: _____
   _____
   _____

   c. With this interaction: _____
   _____
   _____

   d. Learning will be measured by and con-firmed by this method: _____
   _____
   _____

2ND DIMENSION:
The activities are meaningful, energetic, and dramatic.

AND

3RD DIMENSION:
Use interaction to inform, amaze, exercise, apply, and challenge the mind of each student.

This is the teacher's reality check. The Basic Concept identified the first dimension. Now, the Implementation Grid will help establish our second and third dimensions. Fascination requires interaction. It is through student, teacher, idea, and activity interacting that depth of meaning, knowing, probing, wondering, and learning can occur and through that fascination can be ignited. The reality check to confirm that genuine, impactful interaction is occurring is the Interaction Lesson Plan Grid.

This thirty-two-cell grid (Figure 4.5) helps guide creation of or selection of activities and the methods of interacting.

Student Skills	Teacher Skills			
	A **Challenge Students**	**B** **Variety of Teaching Methods**	**C** **Enthusiasm & Encourage-ment**	**D** **Connect Learning with Living**
1. Basics				
2. Communication				
3. Computer Use				
4. Thinking				
5. Problem Solving				
6. Life-long Learning				
7. People Skills				
8. Work Ethic				

Figure 4.5.   Interaction Lesson Plan—Instruction Grid.

The thirty-two-cell Interactive Lesson Plan—Instruction Grid is a quality assurance tool that enables teachers to confirm that the lesson being designed will include the type of interaction that fascinates students and causes learning. For example, "Did the activity I planned challenge students via problem solving, which is cell A-5 on the thirty-two-cell grid? If not, that is OK, but fascinating interaction would be enhanced if each of the four teacher skills are used with each lesson. The student skill(s) matched with the four teacher skills will vary from lesson to lesson, as shown below:

- Lesson for Monday, September 10
  Cells: A-1, B-2, C-5, and D-7
- Lesson for Tuesday, September 11
  Cells: A-8, B-3, C-6, and D-4

The six-part sequence borrowed from athletics can help a teacher arrange the ideas, activities, and methods that were identified with the Basic Concept and the Instruction Grid. The Basic Concept helps identify the first dimension and the Instruction Grid helps identify the second and third dimensions of fascinating three-dimensional teaching. The six-part sequence helps arrange the many activities in three-dimensional teaching.

Fascination can be created. All students can learn and at high levels. All teachers can teach and at great levels. Fascination, learning, and great teaching do not just happen; rather, they are caused. School cannot merely be a continuation of what has always been done before in school. Teaching cannot just be last year's lessons recopied with this year's copy machine.

If teachers plan and design each lesson as precisely as the best coaches plan and design each practice and game plan for each game, classrooms can become more productive, more meaningful, more fascinating places where the purpose of a school—to cause learning—is pursued with the same mutual commitment of students and teachers that athletes and coaches share and with the same mutual fascination that athletes and coaches have toward their shared goals and dreams.

Reflection

The following questions can help a teacher think through the overall process and purpose of creating fascinating lessons. Please reflect on these questions.

(1) How can teachers and students actually *do* math, science, language arts, social studies, and other subjects rather than just imitate, look at, read about, or hear about those topics? Note: Some reading and hearing will be needed, but teaching and learning need to be more than reading and listening.

(2) How can the classroom be active, vibrant, imaginative, and innovative rather than passive, sedate, mundane, and boring?

Note: There are times when silence is needed and pencil and paper work is done, but teaching and learning need to be more than those activities.

(3) How can learning be experienced, internalized, made worthwhile, and made meaningful rather than well, ya know, I mean, sorta absorbed because students slightly remember something they heard or read or watched?

(4) How can the classroom be a place that matters and has experiences that matter rather than a place and experiences that must be endured?

(5) How can other parts of life that fascinate students—sports, music, relationships, growing up, money, concerts, entertainment, television, movies, food—offer ideas and methods that can be used in the classroom?

(6) If I were the typical student, would the lesson I have planned for my students to experience today fascinate me?

(7) Am I "covering material" or "causing learning"? Classroom clerks cover material. Teachers cause learning.

(8) Am I doing teaching the way I hope my students are doing studying, learning, and studenting?

The Faculty Lounge Perspective

We've heard from Jared, Heather, and Owen. Now, the conversation in a faculty lounge becomes part of our journey through school. There are stereotypes of teachers, such as the energetic, work 16 hours per day crusader or the lazy, work 0 hours per day salary thief (this teacher shows up, puts in time, but does no real work). There are teachers who accept responsibility for their students succeeding in school while other teachers make excuses.

Amid the gossip and the complaining, the friendly conversations about topics outside of school and the daily reports on people, what is said in a faculty lounge at a school is part of the school's reality. Let's listen to these teachers as they enjoy their duty-free lunch.

Mr. Harvey: Here we go again. The principal must have attended some hot-shot conference in the summer, and now we have to change everything this year. I can't wait to retire in 3 years.

Ms. Hawkins: My lesson plans are good. My students do OK. The ones who flunk are always going to flunk. They don't care about school. Their families just blame us for their problems. Do those parents ever come to school?

Ms. Hamlyn: I'd like to find ways to help the students who fail, but who has the time. We have our own families to take care of. There are always papers to grade or meetings to attend. How can we make up new lesson plans? Who has the time?

Mr. Keegan: What do you people do to students who complain about the work you give them to do as much as you complain about the work we are told to do. All of us got information in June from the principal about the way we should change lesson plans. He had three meetings this summer so you could attend one at your convenience. If you wasted the summer, that's your fault.

Ms. Hamlyn: I had things to do this summer. I'm not paid to work on school all summer.

Mr. Keegan: So you figure that teaching is an 8-hour per day job only on days that students come to school or that teachers come for work days. The rest of the time is free time, I guess. But you get paid a full-time salary.

Ms. Kaymen: Why is everyone so angry? The school year is just starting, and we're already into the faculty lounge wrestling match. If you have a complaint, go see the principal. If all of your students are already making straight A's in all classes, great, but even those students deserve the best challenge we can give. Why not try what we are being told to do?

Mr. Harvey: Nice try, Ms. Kaymen. I've been here a lot longer than you. New ideas come and go. Principals come and go. I give my students what has always worked. They keep quiet and do their assignments or they keep quiet and do nothing. I insist on the quiet. It's their choice to work or not.

Mr. Brown: Mr. Harvey, there are recent college graduates who could not find teaching jobs this summer because people like you don't know when to get out of the way. I'll never understand why you think it is fair to teach students today exactly the way you taught their parents. Everything else in society has changed except you. It's not right to use nineteenth-century methods to teach twentieth-century information to twenty-first-century students.

Mr. Harvey: Brown, it's people like you who give us wild ideas like the new math or open classrooms or touchy-feely sensitivity training. Get real, man. Quit falling for every fad in education.

Ms. Cassidy: Take it easy, guys. You two will never agree. Now what can we do about these lunches? Is this the best our school can offer?

Ms. MacCull: Bring your own lunch if this is not good enough, or I could share my all natural health food delights I brought. Yogurt, anyone?

Ms. Sherrill: Listen to us. We argue. We talk about silly things. There is an issue here. The students were excited on the first day of school. They were glad to be here. One week later, and we're all back in the same ruts. The good students behave and turn in work. The average students get by. The students who will fail this year have already made it obvious who they are. Our job is to teach all of them. Why can't we keep them as excited about school as they were on the first day?

Mr. Harvey: Because what they were excited about then was seeing their friends. It was a reunion. Now the cliques are back together. The habits are there. Nothing changes.

Ms. Jay: I've listened to all of this, and there is one conclusion— we're cheating the students. We're the adults. It is our job to get them excited about school. It is our job to teach all of them. If we have to do something new that is more work, that's just the way it is. No wonder the public is not satisfied with schools. We ask for more money, but we aren't willing to do the work that gets the results the taxpayers deserve.

Mr. Harvey: OK, Mr. Brown. Ms. Jay, what do you suggest we do?

Mr. Brown: Well, the faculty lounge at lunch is not the place or the time to make official decisions. Still, I'd suggest that we ask for a formal faculty meeting to present all ideas about the new lesson plan process. Some teachers came to school ready to use the plan. I hear good news from them. Other teachers have ignored the instructions we were given. If our students do that, we punish them. If we can get the adults here to do their jobs correctly, most things will work out.

Mr. Harvey: Great idea. We can use that meeting to tell the principal exactly what we think. This lesson plan idea will never last past that meeting.

Ms. Jay: See you at the next meeting Mr. Harvey.

Ms. Keegan: It's almost time to go get our students. Is anyone staying for cheerleading try-outs today? I volunteered to help, and I was hoping I would have some company.

Ms. Kaymen: I'm staying. See you there.

What are the most important conclusions that the faculty lounge conversation suggests? There are many (please add your own):

(1) The work ethic among teachers is quite varied.

(2) The understanding of a teacher's job description also is quite varied among teachers.

(3) Teachers bring many attitudes, expectations, habits, strengths, and limitations to work with them each day.

(4) Educational innovation and change will usually have skeptics and will usually be met with a range from rejection to acceptance to support.

(5) Faculty lounge conversations are not official school policy-making or decision-making processes.

(6) Teachers may think that what they are doing is OK, even if what they are doing is vastly different from what other teachers are doing. The range of what teachers think is OK teaching is probably wider than the range of what really is good teaching.

(7)

(8)

(9)

(10)

School Purpose

If the teachers in that faculty lounge discussion were asked, "What is the purpose of our school?" what answers could be expected? The likelihood that different answers would be given indicates a problem. How can an organization fully succeed if its members are moving in different ways toward different goals in pursuit of different purposes?

Workers who come to a car assembly plant bring different attitudes, work ethics, and personalities; however, the purpose of the car assembly plant, the car company, and the employees is to manufacture a quality car that will provide safe, reliable transportation to the owner of the car.

Employees of a restaurant come from varied family situations, educational backgrounds, or personal experiences, but they all have duties to complete at work so the purpose of the restaurant—to serve quality food at reasonable prices in a pleasant setting—can be fulfilled.

Is it easier to manufacture cars or to prepare meals than it is to teach students? Each of those endeavors could merit a list of reasons that put it in the difficult category, but all these can be done with superior results. There are great cars, great restaurants, and great schools. One advantage these great manufacturers, business workers, or educators give themselves is a clear statement of purpose coupled with a relentless, undivided commitment to that purpose.

The purpose of a school is to cause learning.

Children and teenagers are more likely to commit themselves to something fascinating than to something boring.

To increase the commitment that children and teenagers make toward learning at school, school can make its learning experiences more fascinating.

If the reader is realistic, a question is starting to emerge—can every lesson be fascinating? The answer is yes. Details will come from the case study below.

Case Studies in Lesson Planning: Ideas to Cause Learning

A teacher needs to cause her students to learn what the idea/concept "1/2" means. What activities in a classroom could be used to help the students learn what "1/2" is? The list below is started for you, but please complete it with more ideas:

(1) Use money—2 half-dollars and a dollar bill; 2 quarters and a half dollar.

(2) Use food—divide a pizza into halves; divide another, smaller pizza into halves.

(3) Use paper, pencil, rulers, scissors to cut papers into equal halves.

(4) Use sports—what is half-time of a game? What happened before half-time? What happens after half-time? How much of the game was played before half-time? How much of the game will be played after half-time?

(5) Use age—What does it mean to be 8 1/2 years old?

(6) "Here's a worksheet about what 1/2 is. Read this, answer the questions, and hand it in."

(7) Divide the students into two groups, each group equal in number of students. Re-assemble the total group into one whole. Divide again into halves.

(8) "Today, I'll explain what 1/2 is. Listen to me. Half is more than nothing, but is less than one. It is in the middle."

(9) "Who can explain what 1/2 means?"

(10)

(11)

(12)

(13)

(14)

(15)

There are other activities that could be created. Keep thinking of ways to cause students to learn what 1/2 is using these skills or resources:

(16) Computer—

(17) Problem solving—

(18) Communications—

(19) The school building—

(20) The classroom walls—

What happens if the students stand by each other to form a human line that goes from the middle of the back wall in the classroom to the middle of the front wall of the classroom? How could a teacher use this activity to teach 1/2?

Some learning could be caused from each activity on the above list. A conscientious teacher may include several if not many different activities to make sure that all students are thoroughly learning. When selecting activities from a list of options, keep in mind each of the three dimensions of fascinating teaching: (1) the various activities need to be purposefully planned. This means that more than one activity is used and that all activities are planned—they are thought through in advance, and all preparations are made prior to class. This also means that activities are chosen because they best cause learning—that is the purpose; (2) the activities are meaningful, energetic, and dramatic. Half of a pizza is more dramatic than problems 1–10 on a worksheet; although doing both may be the best plan; (3) the activities enable the teacher and the students to have much interpersonal interaction and intellectual interaction to challenge each mind and to create a depth of knowing. Also, the activities are arranged in a sequence that builds competence and interest.

The next example is for a teacher whose students need to learn how candidates for president of the United States are selected. The list below will include as many activities as the reader and the author can create. The goal is to cause learning that fascinates the student—or, to so fascinate the student that learning is caused. Some activities listed by the author intentionally do not pass the fascination test, so read this list carefully.

(1) Watch historical documentary films about this subject.

(2) Read books such as Theodore White's *The Making of the President* series.

(3) "Read Chapter 6 in the textbook, and answer the questions at the end of each section and at the end of the chapter."

(4) Interview local, state, or national political activists.

(5) Tape broadcasts from C-SPAN or CNN to watch in class.

(6) Play a simulation game about presidential elections.

(7) Divide the class into groups to research how the selection process for U.S. presidential candidates has changed.

(8) Assign one student group this topic—how presidential candidates should be selected—and contrast that with the system that is used.

(9) Involve the whole school in a simulated process of presidential primary elections, nominating conventions, and a general election. Complete this with a presidential inauguration ceremony.

(10) Use the Internet to obtain daily updates from political parties, candidates, and interest groups.

(11) Use the worksheets provided by the textbook publisher to go with the chapter in the book about presidential elections.

(12) Use materials from 5 or 10 years ago that your students were given then and you have extra copies of.

(13) Spend a day in the library so the students can research the topic.

(14) Have students call ten people at random—give each student a different page from the phone book to avoid duplication—and conduct a survey to see what local people know about the presidential candidate selection process.

(15) During a presidential election year, subscribe to several newspapers from outside your state to see how elections are reported elsewhere.

(16) Have students contrast the U.S. candidate selection process with the systems other countries use for selecting potential leaders.

(17)

(18)

(19)

(20)

(21)

Think outside of the box of typical, ordinary activities. New is not always better. Old is not always bad. The goal is to cause learning. Consider every possible activity, method, and resource, and then use those that will cause the most and the best learning, that will cause the most and the best fascination, that will create three-dimensional teaching and learning, that will enhance interaction, that will enhance instructional intensity, and that will enhance intellectual intensity.

Reverse. Shift gears. Now let's intentionally create a very boring lesson. Let's put ourselves in the role of being the world's most boring teacher who has led students into the abyss of intellectual apathy. The subject of the lesson is science, and the purpose of the lesson is to cause learning about nutritional foods that also taste great.

How to Create a Boring Lesson about Nutritional Foods

(1) Come to class completely unprepared. "Uh, what are we doing today? You can talk quietly while I get ready."

(2) Come to class late.

(3) Come to class angry about something at home.

(4) At the start of class say, "What we are doing today is not very important, but the principal told me I have to cover this topic before those state tests are given next month."

(5) Tell the students that you really do not know much about this topic.

(6) Use old, outdated, no longer accurate hand-out materials.

(7) "Turn to page 78. Read the chapter. Write an outline of the chapter. Work silently on your own. Turn that in tomorrow. We'll see a filmstrip then, and you'll take a test the next day."

(8) Give weak responses to questions from students. "Well, some junk food is kind of nutritious. Some healthy food is sort of junkie. I guess it's different for different people."

(9) Lecture. Ignore questions. Stand in the front of the classroom and never move around. Never use the chalkboard, overhead, pictures, or other audio-visual materials. Use a monotone voice.

(10) Even though the subject is food, do not bring any food samples to the classroom.

(11) Let every student leave class if they ask for permission to go anywhere.

(12)

(13)

(14)

(15)

(16)

The students who were taught by teachers using only the methods on the list above are bored students. Some of them may comply, do the work, and avoid both trouble and a bad grade. Some or many of the other students will use this teacher and this class as further evidence that school is boring and meaningless.

When Teachers Were Bored

Teachers can relate to these bored students more closely than it may appear. How many teachers have had to attend in-service, professional development, or other training programs that were absolutely worthless in content and boring in presentation? Those programs should have been better and could have been fascinating; instead, they amounted to "putting in hours" and "covering material."

Other programs that teachers have attended did captivate and fascinate. Perhaps a civic club had a speaker who inspired you. What did that speaker do that you could duplicate in your classroom? Perhaps a movie, a book, a Broadway show, or a church service fascinated you. How could the methods used there be brought to your classroom? Think.

The most fascinating (pick one or two):

_____ class

_____ speaker

_____ concert

_____ theatrical production

_____ book

_____ church service

_____ community group meeting

_____ movie, television program, video

_____ athletic competition

_____ hobby

_____ training session

_____ sales presentation

_____ television commercial

_____ newspaper or magazine article

_____ CD-ROM

_____ Internet page or web site

_____ computer software

_____ song

_____ other

I ever experienced was on

Date   _____

Place   _____

It was, or they were, fascinating for these reasons:

(1)

(2)

(3)

(4)

(5)

I could apply those reasons and the experiences I had in my classroom by using these methods and activities:

(1)

(2)

(3)

(4)

(5)

Conduct the same fascination survey with your students. What has fascinated them? What could a teacher borrow from those experiences that fascinated the students to help make the classroom a fascinating place where learning is caused and boredom is gone?

One area that some students will mention is sports. As spectators, as participants, as fans, as would-be or wanna-be professional athletes, our society is fascinated by sports. Children, teenagers, and adults eagerly learn sports statistics and anticipate the next sports update on the news.

Borrowing Ideas from a Rarely Reformed Part of School

Following ideas that coaches use at sports practices is the basis for the six-part sequence in this book. Further symbiotic connections between sports and schools are presented below.

Amid the discussion about schools and the education of our young people, there has been little or no concern expressed regarding the athletic talent or performance of our youth. Reading, writing, and SAT scores may be weak, but students seem to do well with touchdowns, free throws, and home runs.

There are simple reasons for this athletic success. Schools, similar to other organizations, get what they work on best and reward most. Students succeed in athletics for many reasons including the following:

(1) They practice many hours each day.

(2) Crowds, including parents, spend money and time to attend games and to offer enthusiastic support.

(3) Coaches and assistant coaches are carefully chosen.

(4) Coaches are paid for their extra work plus they often are admired, respected, and supported.

(5) Television, radio, and newspapers cover school sporting events.

(6) Big banquets are held to present big awards to athletes.

(7) Students attend summer camps to improve their sports skills.

(8) Sports thrive on competition, keeping score, and giving rewards.

(9) Athletic success is rewarded, rewarded, and rewarded by everything from fame to scholarships, from letter jackets to the chance of a $1 million contract.

Perhaps the academic side of education can learn something from the athletic side. Perhaps some simple changes could cost less than hundreds of millions of dollars, the estimated price tag of educational reform in many states. The simple changes could get equal or better results than the high-priced plan.

(1) Football teams practice in the summer for a month before their first game. Perhaps a few August twice-a-day spelling, reading, and writing practices would get our students ready for their first day of a new school year. Hire a teacher as spelling coach and get started.

(2) Parents and other interested citizens—for every athletic event you attend at a school, make yourself attend a class at the school. Spend a day at school and cheer for students who excel. Offer encouragement to those who struggle. You would do it for a half-back, why not do it for a math student?

(3) Superintendents and principals—put as much effort into recruiting and selecting teachers as you do into finding coaches. The English vacancy on the faculty should cause you as much or more concern as the basketball coaching vacancy.

(4) We pay coaches for the extra work they do with athletics, and they earn that money. Let's pay teachers for the time they spend after school giving special help to students.

(5) Media—you eagerly carry sport scores and stories. You give attention to the naming of a new high school coach. Come on, cover the hiring of a new science teacher. Reporters are sent to sporting events. Send them to academic events, also, and give that an occasional special section in the news, just as you do sports.

(6) Sports banquets are often held to honor the touchdown makers or the home-run hitters. Honors banquets for academic work are less frequent or are less elaborate. Administrators and local government leaders will come present a ring to a state championship football team. Where are those people when the academic awards are presented? Every school has an Athletic Director. How many have Academic Directors?

(7) Parents spend much money to send Johnny to basketball camp or Julie to tennis camp in the summer. Let's have spelling camps, writing camps, and math

camps. Schools could employ some teachers for an extra week in the summer to run these camps, which parents or guardians pay for.

(8) Sports are exciting because of competition and because of keeping score. Let's teach with the same exciting concepts such as

- Every correct answer all week in a classroom earns the student a chance to register for a prize given away on Friday. Local businesses will need to help by donating prizes. This method is known to build radio station audiences, and it is known to increase student attention, effort, and learning.

- Trivia—ask questions in the classroom using a game-show style. The student answering the most questions wins, maybe an apple. Every correct answer earns each student registration in the bonus drawing for a prize or for extra credit.

- Four-Minute Drill—all of your classes are asked the same questions. The class that can answer the most correctly in 4 minutes is the winner. Get or make a simple scoreboard to use.

(9) Capitalism—athletes are rewarded. Workers are rewarded. The possibility of a reward can help create a drive to do better and to do more. Students can be receptive to the same concept. "Everyone who can name the fifty states correctly on a map this Friday wins a piece of candy." Students get report cards four times a year. Would adults be satisfied if paychecks came quarterly? Students could benefit from frequent rewards and observations.

Schools can improve when (1) teaching improves and (2) parents are 100% involved in the education of their children. Sure, many teachers deserve more money and a chance to earn bonus pay for superior work. Sure, strict standards for people entering teaching are needed. Yet, teaching remains an intimate, human adventure. More laws and rules could get in the way. Solutions can be simple and direct.

Teachers—make your students practice as hard and as much as any athlete. Then, make your classroom as exciting as any sports activity.

Parents and administrators—support teachers, teaching, and academics the way you support coaches, coaching, and sports. When our students as students receive the care, feeding, and support of our students as athletes, we will see great progress.[1]

This chapter will conclude with the reader creating a fascinating three-dimensional lesson and then with a pep talk. First, the reader selects the topic and the grade level. Use the Basic Concept, the Instruction Grid (Figure 4.5), and the six-part sequence. Emphasize (1) activities that are purposefully planned, (2) activities that have meaning, energy, and drama, and (3) human and intellectual interaction that create great intensity in the classroom. The format to use is the same as that previously presented and reproduced here for convenience:

---

[1]This article was originally printed in the Lexington (Kentucky) *Herald-Leader,* June 12, 1985.

Creating Three-Dimensional Teaching

How to Organize

1ST DIMENSION:
A variety of purposefully planned activities.

Use the Interaction Lesson Plan—Basic Concept:
1. The purpose of this lesson is to cause learning:
   a. Of this idea: _____

   _____

   _____

   b. Through these activities: _____

   _____

   _____

   c. With this interaction: _____

   _____

   _____

   d. Learning will be measured by and confirmed
      by this method: _____

   _____

   _____

2ND DIMENSION:
The activities are meaningful, energetic, and dramatic.

AND

3RD DIMENSION:
Use interaction to inform, amaze, exercise, apply, and challenge the mind of each student.

This is the teacher's reality check. Fascination requires interaction. It is through student, teacher, idea, and activity interacting that depth of meaning, knowing, probing, wondering, and learning can occur and through that fascination can be ignited. The reality check to confirm that genuine, impactful interaction is occurring is the Interaction Lesson Plan—Instruction Grid.

The thirty-two-cell grid (Figure 4.5, p. 82) helps guide creation of or selection of activities and the methods of interacting.

Use the six-part sequence (see page 48) to add detailed implementation action for parts 1-b and 1-c of the Interaction Lesson Plan, to confirm that the Interaction Lesson Plan is adequately detailed already, and to arrange the order of events. First, we had our overall idea and plan. Second, we created the specific design to implement the instruction and the interaction. Third, we established the sequence that will most enhance learning.

(1) Warm-up:

(2) Drills:

(3) Skills:

(4) Scrimmage:

(5) Cool-down:

(6) Huddle:

Now, check yourself by actually teaching the lesson you created. Ask another teacher or other colleagues to observe. Ask the students for their evaluation. Videotape and/or audiotape the lesson for your review.

Pep Talk

The thoughts that follow are reminders of why we chose teaching or of why teaching chose us.

Why do we teach—to make a difference in the hearts, minds, and souls of young people who need us. There are few better lives to live. In the depths of my heart, mind, and soul, I am a teacher. I need to teach because it is what I do and it is what I am supposed to do. I am a teacher. That word, teacher. There is something about it. Teachers. Teachers. That's it. Perhaps the answer is within the word, teachers.

Look for words within the word teachers. Using the letters t, e, a, c, h, e, r, and s certainly can create words that are the essential parts of being a real, great teacher.

Teach: Above all, my job is to teach. I cause learning. If I were a sales representative and I presented my products, but no person bought, I would not have succeeded in sales. I would have talked and presented, but not sold. If a teacher talks and makes presentations in class, but students do not learn, teaching did not happen. A teacher teaches, causes learning, and gets results from everyone.

Each: The salesman has the luxury of not having to make a sale to everyone. If half of his customers buy, he and his company can make a fine profit. The teacher has to get through to each student. Great teachers keep each student working, learning, and paying attention. Anything below 100% is not good enough—it could be good, but it is not good enough. One hundred percent is the standard for a great teacher. If 110% is possible, then let's shoot for that.

Share: Teaching is win-win. It is not a court case where one side will win and the other loses. The teacher and the student win together or they both lose. If we share our time, energy, heart, ideas, and determination with the students, they will respond by sharing their time, energy, heart, ideas, and determination. Their response may be slow in coming, and it may begin in a small way, but a great teacher's persistence will get a response.

Reach: Reach for the stars, for every student making an A on the report card, for no words being spelled incorrectly, for perfect behavior, and for every moment being worthwhile, productive, important, and fascinating.

Ache: Teaching hurts. It hurts when the student you worked with flunks the test. It hurts when a student gets killed in a car crash after a graduation party. It hurts when a parent yells at you in public. It hurts when you get hate mail. It hurts when your car or house is vandalized by silly youngsters. It hurts physically at the end of a rugged week. Hang in there. Go back each day and work harder, work smarter, care more deeply, and get new results. The joy of your effort will cause the students to learn and then the ache will be reduced, although it may never completely go away.

Hear: How desperately the students want someone to listen to them, to pay attention to them, and to confide in them or with them. The great teacher has to hear what is not spoken—the students may show their needs, but they may not always verbally express them. Take the time to hear what they are saying in words, expressions, their clothes, their music, and their actions. Hear them, and respond with proper concern be it a smile, a punishment, a talk, or a call home.

Tears: You will cry. There will be tears of sadness if the child gets arrested. There will be tears of joy when they graduate and then when they come back to tell you about their jobs, their weddings, or their graduate school scholarships. You will cry when you see a child who was abused at home. You may cry when a child says, "Thank you. You really helped me." Let the tears come, they are a part of the process of caring.

Heart: Love the students. Love them every minute of every day. Love them by putting your total effort and your best effort into each bulletin board you make, the homework papers you grade, and the special time you allow for conversations with them at lunch when you visit students instead of segregating yourself with adults at the teachers' table or in the faculty lounge.

Share your heart with them, open yourself up to them—keep a few secrets, but let a bit of the real you come through. Love the students a lot, and then love them some more. Be demanding because that is a high form of love. Do not let them take advantage of your fondness for them. When they fail you or let you down, you may decide to give them a second chance, but do not be a pushover.

Search: Life does not yet make sense to the students. They are searching through English, math, science, history; through boy meets girl and girl meets boy; through sports, band, clubs, and competition. Join them in their search. Be their partner. Be interested in their activities and in their ideas and in them. Let them join you in the search to become a great teacher.

Act: Two meanings from this word apply. One, act in the sense of take action. You have to do something to make learning occur. Do something special, something difficult, exciting, important, worthwhile, proper, and productive. Do something different from what you did last year. Never let a minute pass as you wait for a bell. Act, ask questions, play trivia, do something to exercise their minds.

Two, act in the sense of perform. The classroom is your stage, and you have a lovely audience. Prepare your script, but be open to improvisation. Rehearse your lines, know your material, and never try to wing it with no preparation. Act, be dramatic, be funny, be bold, artistic, occasionally unpredictable, and always fascinating.

Chapter 5 will concentrate on the inevitable reality—despite our best preparation, the finest lesson planning, the most relentless effort, and our teaching that has every ingredient of three-dimensional fascination, some students are defiant.

Fascinating Lessons as a Way to Inspire Students

Including Defiant, Stubborn, Apathetic Students

Some students defy all teachers. Those students are few and cannot be allowed to shape what teachers do or to shape teachers' perspectives of their job.

Most defiant students can be won over by a determined, capable teacher.

All students deserve to be taught in the most productive and the most fascinating ways that cause learning.

This chapter addresses the reality of defiant, stubborn, and apathetic students. This book also acknowledges that some teachers have become defiant, stubborn, and apathetic, but that those teachers can be shown ways to increase their effectiveness and, therefore, their job satisfaction. When adults do their duty correctly, the results can be amazing.

Yes, some students do need to be assigned to alternative programs, alternative schools, or boot camps. These students are a small minority and are not the emphasis of this book; however, some of the ideas in this book could apply in those alternative settings. One of the many reasons that some students have become so disruptive in school could be that school was absolutely boring and meaningless to them.

STUDENTS ARE REAL PEOPLE LIVING REAL LIVES

"DO you love students?" asked the very serious principal as the first question in any interview with a prospective teacher. A yes answer was followed by the full battery of questions. A no answer resulted in a shortened interview and zero consideration for the job.

The principal who told the author of that interviewing method is known as an educator who lives for students, works for students, and who loves students. He also demands that students make a total commitment to school. The teachers are expected to constantly demonstrate their total commitment to students.

"Do you like students? Do you like being with children and teenagers?" Those questions reveal as much or more than the "love" question. Liking the students does not mean retreating to one's youth and being their friend; rather, liking means that you are glad to be together, you value the time together, and you actually miss the students during vacation.

More than love or like are these challenges: (1) can you accept the students as real people who are living real lives and (2) can you teach them in ways that cause them to learn and to be fascinated with learning?

MORE FROM THE FACULTY LOUNGE

The responses from teachers to those challenges vary. A return to the faculty lounge can help provide some insight. After hearing the teachers, a conversation from students in the cafeteria will be presented. It is interesting to notice this irony—teachers gather in the faculty lounge to talk about students sometimes while across the hall in the cafeteria students sometimes are talking about teachers. What could happen if the two groups talked with each other, listened to each other and found some new understanding? Upon such hopes, some of us eagerly arrive at school early every morning still believing in the dream that originally brought us to this vital work we call teaching.

Ms. Hamlyn: Is anyone going to that conference this weekend? I think it is about getting parents more involved in school. If they don't get themselves involved in school, what can we do about it?

Ms. Hawkins: I heard about that conference. We've all been through presentations like that. Everything is our fault. The students are victims of a system that ignores their needs and their individualities. Get real. Every student at our school is given the opportunity each day to learn and to avoid trouble. Parents can come up here and get involved right now. Who needs to waste time at that conference?

Ms. MacCull: It's not like you have to go. If we go to the conference this weekend, there is a mandatory training session later in the year that we are excused from. You have a choice. Why complain about that?

Mr. Harvey: MacCull, if we don't complain about silly conferences like this, people will think we want more of them. I'm not going either, but I want the principal to know that it is silly to even offer this option. The people putting on the conference don't know us or our school. Who needs them?

Mr. Keegan:	I'm going. Every teacher in this school would like for more parents to get more involved. Here's a chance to learn how that could be done. It's 3 hours on Saturday morning, and the conference provides child care. There is no cost to any teacher, plus they provide breakfast and they give you printed materials to bring back to school. I'll be glad to tell everyone about it on Monday.
Ms. Kaymen:	Please get an extra set of materials for me. I'd like to go, but the children have soccer on Saturday morning.
Ms. Jay:	Here's what interests me about the conference. It is about getting parents more involved in school, but what really matters is getting students more involved in school. I know that the parents can be a great source of help to us, but when a student really gets turned on about school, everything starts to happen the way it should. We can reach the students each day. We may never get any response from some parents.
Mr. Harvey:	Hey, MacCull, how's the health food? The cafeteria did a good job today with the pizza and the breadsticks. You can eat those, can't you?
Ms. MacCull:	Mr. Harvey, maybe we can send you to a conference about nutrition, but let's not change the subject. Ms. Jay is right. Are we doing everything right here at school to impact each student in the best possible way? Simple things, like speaking to a student who seems to always be alone or finding out why a student who has been absent for a few days is not here, maybe even calling him or her or going to his or her home.
Ms. Hamlyn:	Who has time for that? The secretaries and the school counselors can do that. I have classes to work on.
Ms. Jay:	It is amazing how much time you can save if you do things like that. Taking an interest in a student who is absent may encourage the student to attend school more. Then you don't have to spend all that time helping them get caught up. You know the habit we get into—there's always time to do it over, but why wasn't there time to do it right in the first place?
Ms. Sherrill:	We should cover the walls in this faculty lounge with pictures of all of our students at this school. It could help us remember why we are here. We aren't here for anything except to help each student learn all he or she can learn. If we are here for any other reason, something is wrong.

The principal, Mr. Francis, had just walked into the faculty lounge to get his lunch from the refrigerator.

Mr. Francis: Great idea. We have pictures left from the yearbook. Could you get those, Ms. Sherrill, and cover the walls in here? Some students could help you one day before school or after school. If you need anything, please tell me.

Ms. Sherrill: Sure. We'll get it done immediately. Thanks for your support, Mr. Francis.

Mr. Harvey: Can you believe that? Even when we come in here for lunch we are going to be looking at the students.

Ms. Jay: Maybe it will help you remember that the reason for school is students, not lunch. That may sound harsh, but come on Mr. Harvey, you come in here each day and complain. There are all of those 22- and 23-year-olds who would do anything to be hired here to teach. You've got all your years of experience and your tenure and can you honestly claim that you are making sure that each student learns all that they can?

Mr. Harvey: Ms. Jay, I know your type. You work hard for a few years and get noticed, and then you wear out. I may be slow and steady, but I've lasted longer in this work than you have thought about.

Ms. Kaymen: Hey, when our students talk to each other like that, we send them to conflict resolution. The adults need to set the example. It's time to go anyway. Ms. Sherrill, if you need some help getting those pictures put up in here, let me know. That was a great idea.

How many of the people in that faculty lounge conversation are totally devoted to students? How many of them are eager to be devoted to students but, after some years of problems with bureaucracies, angry parents, defiant students, legal mandates, and too many meaningless teacher training sessions, have just reduced themselves to the lowest acceptable level of doing their job, getting paid, and letting off steam in the faculty lounge? How many of them see the inconsistency between what they expect students to think, do, say, and believe and what they as faculty members think, do, say, and believe in some revealing moments?

What happens to the conscientious teachers who are surrounded by colleagues who complain, make excuses, and never are satisfied? How are the serious problems separated from the silly gripes?

One answer to those questions is "total and constant dedication to causing learning?" If everything done, said, approved, rejected, or discussed at a school is based upon the purpose of a school—to cause learning—some, if not all, of the wasted effort, such as faculty lounge banter, could be eliminated.

How do educators create a school in which there is total and constant dedication to causing learning? One answer is that you make the school, the classrooms, and the learning so fascinating that students, teachers, and staff members are completely caught up in the purpose of the school. There is no need to, and there is no time to do anything but cause learning in schools, which are totally and constantly dedicated to causing learning.

What about the teachers who do not pull their own weight? Why were they hired to start with? It is too late to "unhire" them, but they can be given very specific directives, in writing, about what must happen in their classroom and in their conduct at school. If they improve, great; if they do not improve, they are taken through the consequences of conduct unbecoming a professional, insubordination, or whatever the category of defiance was. Termination is possible.

What about teachers who are willing to improve, but who do not know how to make their classrooms and their students fascinating? Chapter 6 will provide more details about the professional development and teacher training aspects of making learning at school fascinating, but here's an encouraging note—even those people who are certain that they were "born to teach" seek ways to become better teachers; therefore, any teacher can learn how to be a better teacher.

MORE PERSPECTIVE FROM STUDENTS

What were the students doing while their teachers had lunch in the faculty lounge? They were having lunch across the hallway, and they were having their typical conversation. Let's listen.

Owen: Did your brother get his driver's license, Heather?

Heather: Barely. He made some mistake and almost flunked, but he got it. He has to pay for his car insurance now. He'll go broke, but he thinks it's going to be nothing but fun to drive.

Owen: My sister said the best thing that happened to her in high school was getting her driver's license. After that, she had more friends than ever. She got her license before most people in her grade, so that was cool.

Jared: Did you hear about that new law? When we are 16, we can only get the temporary kind of license. We have to practice for something like 6 months before we can get a real license. It used to be just 1 month. That's no fair.

Heather:	Well, talk to Mr. Prather about it. He probably knows how you could express your ideas to people in charge.
Jared:	Yeah, Mr. Prather would tell me all he could, but that law is not going to change. Some adults are just out to make things tough for us. They probably don't want 16-year-olds to drive at all.
Owen:	Hey, I heard that one of the teachers got a ticket for speeding. He was late to school and was doing something like 55 miles per hour in a neighborhood. He has a huge fine to pay and may have to go to some class. Pretty funny, huh?
Jared:	Who was it? I hope it was Mr. Harvey. He deserves it.
Heather:	Hey, what are you guys doing this weekend? There is a movie I want to see. Anyone want to go?
Owen:	How are we going to get there?
Heather:	It's not that far. We can walk. Call me after school. Hey, maybe we could ask that new guy to go with us. I talked with him yesterday. Is that OK?
Jared:	Uh, well, we really don't know him.
Owen:	Jared means that he does not want any other guy hanging out with you, Heather.
Jared:	Shut up, Owen. At least people want to hang out with me. Who was the last girl who liked you?
Heather:	I know who it is. Janet is crazy about you, Owen. Don't you ever notice her? She looks at you all day.
Owen:	Yeah, right. Janet just broke up with some high-school guy. He'd destroy me if I went out with his old girlfriend.
Heather:	Call her. It can't hurt. There's Ms. Hamlyn. The teachers must think lunch is over, but we have 5 more minutes. Hey, is there any homework due for our next class, Jared?
Jared:	Uh, I think so. Didn't we have to prepare a television-type news story? I saw something on the news last night, and I think I can fake the rest of it.
Heather:	Maybe we could do it together. I forgot about that. Hurry up and tell me about it. OK?
Jared:	Yeah, it was about the president and his wife, I think. Hey, we could pretend to be them and answer questions from the class. That would impress Ms. Jay. She loves it when everyone gets involved.
Heather:	Yeah, OK, let's practice. Owen, ask us a question.
Owen:	OK. Who is the boss between you two?

While Heather, Jared, and Owen had lunch, there were hundreds of other conversations going on in the cafeteria. The students talked about everything from each other to sports, from the weekend plans to food, from teachers to television. Most of the conversations did not deal with academics, until a student realized that some homework was due in a few minutes. Most of the conversations were typical, friendly, and social—that's fine. Some of the conversations or the behavior may start a problem, and the cafeteria supervisors will need to prevent or stop that.

What is revealed from the conversation that Heather, Jared, and Owen had? Try this—that they are real people who are living real lives. Laws about driver's licenses impact these three teenagers. Getting to the movies is a problem that needs to be resolved. Being ready for class, that is real, too. Their opinions of teachers reflect what they see at school and how they see it.

FASCINATING OPPORTUNITIES EVERYWHERE

What could help build the commitment that Heather, Jared, Owen, and other students have toward school? Well, how fascinating is the cafeteria? What? The question is—how fascinating is the cafeteria? For that matter, how fascinating are the hallways and the front hall and the office and every other part of the building?

How many restaurants are decorated to appear as ordinary as the typical school cafeteria? Don't most restaurants try to create some atmosphere? What about other businesses or offices? Some places really amaze you with their design or their decor. Are schools like that? Do schools use the art talent of students to decorate the cafeteria, the hallways, and the office? Do we cover the walls with pictures of students, with displays that recognize great work, with information, with trivia questions that actually relate to school topics, with today's newspaper, with job applications, and with other material that is of interest to students and that can help cause learning?

Having visited some teachers and some students during their lunch, we join them back in the classroom. There is something that is immediately apparent—Heather, Jared, and Owen, along with most students in the cafeteria, were very energetic at lunch. They were paying total attention to their conversations. They were intense about the topics they discussed. They were fascinated about a driver's license. Heather, Jared, and Owen can be intellectually intense. They can be fascinated about important, useful, meaningful topics.

The lunch visit is a reminder that students are real people who are living real lives. The lunch visit also is a reminder about the wide range of work ethic and personal motivation that will be found among teachers. Teachers are also real people who are living real lives, plus they have a real contractual obligation to successfully complete a job. The lunch visit also increased awareness that there are some simple, no-cost, or low-cost opportunities to create, build, and support a school atmosphere of fascination.

A CLASSROOM VISIT—IDEAS TO REMEMBER

Our next stop is in a classroom. The purpose of this visit will be to fully explore the dynamics of preparing a fascinating lesson, teaching that lesson, interacting with all students during that lesson, and evaluating the results of the lesson.

Please keep these thoughts in mind:

(1) Students are real people living real lives.

(2) Much of school seems to be unreal to many students.

(3) Much of what students are supposed to learn at school is boring to many students.

(4) How students are taught is boring to many students.

(5) If school provides students with opportunities to learn and to apply ideas, subjects, and skills that are fascinating and that are learned in fascinating ways, learning at school becomes fascinating.

(6) Reality is fascinating—make school real, and you do a lot to make learning at school fascinating. One measure of real is "What do I do with it now?" meaning what do I do with what we are studying today? How does it make me better today? How does it apply to me, right now?

(7) If a teacher cannot answer a student's questions of "Why do we have to do this?" or "Why do we have to learn this?" with more than "Because it is in the textbook" or "Because that is what we always do," then the teacher needs to change what is being taught or find some genuine reason for it to be learned.

(8) When we ask students to learn what school teaches in the way that school teaches it, we are asking them to invest their precious time, abilities, and childhood–teenage years. Those students get one chance to be students—giving them anything less than totally fascinating, completely meaningful, amazingly challenging experiences is unacceptable.

(9) Life is fascinating. School needs to be as fascinating as life itself. To be anything less is to fail at teaching, at schooling, and at being the type of educator we promised ourselves we would be—the very best, the most energetic, the most creative, the one who would touch lives and hearts and minds.

(10) Technology—audio, video, cable, satellite, computer, and other—is making it possible for any person to access any information. The sup-

plies of textbooks, workbooks, libraries, and other materials that made schools the exclusive or the most efficient places for learning to occur are now available via technology to any subscriber of appropriate services. If all the physical materials needed for an education can be beamed into, faxed into, or transmitted into a home, what is the continued benefit of having a school? What can school uniquely offer? School has to be the place where instructional intensity and intellectual intensity are uniquely available through human interaction of teachers and students. It is in creating the experience of fascinating learning via compelling interaction that schools can still provide a unique educational experience, structure, program, and product.

A CLASSROOM VISIT—THE INTERACTION LESSON PLAN BEING USED IN MATH CLASS

Applying the Interaction Lesson Plan—Basic Concept, Instruction Grid, and six-part sequence to create three-dimensional teaching and learning

1ST DIMENSION: A variety of purposefully planned activities.
Note: This was designed using the Basic Concept.

The purpose of this lesson is to cause learning:

a. Of this idea: A math chart can be used in a business to determine the best price to charge for a product.

b. Through these activities:

- The class begins with newspaper advertisements, fast food restaurant coupons, and two television commercials to introduce the use of numbers by businesses to communicate price.

- Each student identifies a recent purchase of food and prices of similar items are compared/contrasted.

- Identical soft drinks bought at different stores are shown, but the retail prices were different. The teacher leads the students in a discussion of the factors that lead to a pricing decision by a retail business/store.

- Each student is given a different set of numbers showing (a) the five different prices a business charged on different days/weeks for the same product; and (b) the number of sales of that product at each price. Each student then charted the five pairs of numbers.

Note: For the purpose of this exercise, the costs to the business per unit did not change, so profit on the first sale was the same as the profit on the tenth sale. The teacher would introduce the ideas of quantity discounts and variable costs through an interdisciplinary unit with the students' social studies teacher later.

- Students wrote a one paragraph explanation of the price that the business should use to both maximize the benefits to the customers and to maximize the benefits to the business.

c. With this interaction:

- Students will put their charts on the chalkboard; if computers are available in the classroom, some students can put their graphs on the screen and print a copy to show the class.
- Students will give a 1/2-minute oral summary of their data and their conclusion about pricing.
- The teacher will ask one question of each student after his or her presentation.
- Students will vote to indicate agreement or disagreement with the pricing conclusion of each student. Where consensus is not reached, inquiry will probe the reasons as the teacher and students discuss this.

d. Learning will be measured by and confirmed by this method:

- Students will turn in their charts and their paragraphs.
- The 1/2-minute presentation and following discussion/questions.

2ND DIMENSION: The activities are meaningful, energetic, and dramatic.

AND

(1) Warm-up: The newspaper advertisements, restaurant coupons, and television commercials will provide warm-up as the ideas of prices, changes in prices, and pricing decisions are introduced.

(2) Drills:

- Students identify their recent food purchases, and prices were compared/contrasted.
- The teacher provides a case study of the same product purchased at different stores for different prices.

3RD DIMENSION:
Use interaction to
inform, amaze,
exercise, apply, and
challenge the mind
of each student.

Note:
(A) This was
designed using the
Instruction Grid
and the six-part
sequence.

(B) This adds to
the Basic Concept
as a teacher uses
the Grid to more
fully develop the
lesson, and this
arranges the flow
of activities using
the six-part
sequence.

- Action: The teacher needs to add an example of what the students will do next, perhaps using data from the school cafeteria or the school concession stand. This example prepares students for the next action.

(3) Skills: Each student calculates the profit numbers for the data given about prices and number of units that were sold at each price.

(4) Scrimmage: The charts are put on the chalkboard and/or computer, discussed, and evaluated (agreed to or not). The teacher will ask a question of each student after he or she explains the chart. Students will question each other.

(5) Cool-down: Action: The teacher will ask students for overall analysis. What ideas seem to appear across many charts that could lead to general concepts about pricing? Were there any results that did not seem believable? Why? The teacher will ask students to explain how using math in this way could help a business owner make better decisions and avoid mistakes.

(6) Huddle: The teacher concludes with an opportunity for the class to extend their learning via application. How could charts apply to school? For example, the teacher could ask, "Is there a pair of factors such as grades and attendance that function as sales and price work?" The teacher could put students in groups to work on this. "I'll give you 2 minutes to think and talk about that in groups of five. You select a spokesperson to tell me your thoughts."

Note: The six-step plan reminded the author to add two actions that he did not include originally in the first dimension using only the Basic Concept form. Also, this lesson may require two class periods—that is fine.

The thirty-two-cell Interaction Lesson Plan—Instruction Grid (presented in Chapter 3 and reproduced here as Figure 5.1) is used by the teacher as a reality check for the math lesson and can help evaluate a lesson plan (a) as

	Teacher Skills			
	A **Challenge Students**	**B** **Variety of Teaching Methods**	**C** **Enthusiasm & Encourage-ment**	**D** **Connect Learning with Living**
Student Skills				
1. Basics				
2. Communication				
3. Computer Use				
4. Thinking				
5. Problem Solving				
6. Life-long Learning				
7. People Skills				
8. Work Ethic				

Figure 5.1.   Thirty-Two-Cell Interaction Lesson Plan—Instruction Grid.

designed and (b) as taught. Some cells are very obviously at use in the design of this lesson:

- A-1: Basic math is used and applied.
- B-2: Students write, present to the class, and discuss.
- B-3: If available, computers were used by some students to create their charts.
- A-4, D-4: The students had to determine the best price to charge and explain their reasoning.
- D-5: Students applied the math calculations and charts to actual, real-life retail businesses.
- D-6: Students were asked to extend math/chart applications to school so they could identify further use of these skills.
- C-7: The pursuit of consensus, if properly guided by the teacher, helps students learn to work together and make decisions together. If consensus is not attained, the students realize that different businesses make different decisions for different reasons and customers are the final judge.

Note: This grid is a useful evaluation of the teacher's effectiveness after the lesson is taught. Did the interaction occur as intended?

Another way to plan a lesson about math charts is this—"Turn to page 46. Read 46 and 47. I'll put some examples on the board while you read. We'll cover the examples. I'll give you a short worksheet to do on your own. Then you'll have odd-numbered problems 1–15 for homework due tomorrow."

While writing this book, the author used 32 minutes to plan and write out the math lesson presented on pages 107–109. Many people may ask, "Who has time to plan like that?" The answer again is conscientious, serious teachers who realize that their job is to cause learning, not merely to cover material, and who realize that if we teach effectively the first time, we can save endless hours or years that would go to remedial work, after-school tutoring, meetings about unsuccessful students, and other corrective actions. Select one: (a) plan for 32 minutes now and teach to cause learning or (b) use last year's lesson plan plus a textbook's homework assignment and watch the predictable results of bored students making the same grades they usually make.

Thinking is more demanding than not thinking; however, life without thinking is mere existence. A teacher who causes learning has accepted a more demanding duty than a teacher who covers material, keeps students busy, and relies on the textbook or the copy machine; however, education without teachers who cause learning is mere schooling—the passage of years in a school building.

Are we seeking students and teachers who do "schooling" or are we seeking students and teachers who interact in fascinating ways to promote thinking and to cause learning?

If we seek thinkers and causers of learning—and we must—then school has to become a fascinated and fascinating laboratory for thinking, doing, creating, exploring, questioning, and learning. Classroom activities and experiences—lessons—can be designed to cause learning and to fascinate and can be implemented to cause learning and to fascinate. The math lesson has been designed for thinking and learning. Now, if implemented well, thinking will occur, and learning will be caused. Let's listen as the teacher and students work.

A CLASSROOM VISIT—THE LESSON, THE TEACHING, AND THE LEARNING

Ms. Crawford: Good morning. This 2-liter soft drink sells for $.99 at the nearby Kroger. It's featured in the Kroger grocery store's current newspaper and television advertisements. I've checked the price on it at nine other stores—gas stations,

	Wal-mart, other grocery stores. The price ranges from $.89 to $1.49. Plus, the price can change from day to day at the same store. Why would different stores have a different price for the same product? Everyone think of a reason.
Michelle:	They have the freedom to charge the price they want to.
Thomas:	Yeah, and I have the right to shop around.
Ms. Crawford:	You're both right. Stores and customers have freedom. Now, why are different stores charging different prices for the same product? Wouldn't there be a perfect price that every store wants to use?
Ashley:	Where I live, the little store always charges too much. That pop bottle would cost $1.49. They know you don't have much choice, so they charge too much, and most people just go along with it.
Jake:	They don't have to go along with it—$1.49 for that bottle of soft drink is too much. If people quit paying the price, the price goes down.
James:	Maybe, but if they thought they were only going to sell a few, they might try to charge the highest possible price.
Ms. Crawford:	Here are some coupons from fast food restaurants: $1.00 off per meal; free coffee when you buy a sandwich; buy one dessert get another for a penny; one pizza for $7.99, two pizzas for $13.99, and three pizzas for $17.99. How do you figure out which restaurant is giving you the best deal?
Emily:	You do the math, plus you figure out what you really need. The price per pizza is best when you buy three, but if you only need one pizza, buying three is a waste of money.
Ms. Crawford:	What does Emily mean when she says that you do the math? (Pause 3 seconds) Mike, what does that mean? [Ms. Crawford moves toward Mike as she continues to constantly walk throughout the classroom keeping in close touch with all students by her presence, a direct glance, or direct conversation.]
Mike:	Uh, I really did not have my hand up, Ms. Crawford.
Ms. Crawford:	But you can answer the question, Mike.
Mike:	Do the math means do the math, like, uh, add and subtract. Work it out. Figure it out.
Ms. Crawford:	Right, Figure it out. That's what math lets us do. Now, watch these two television commercials, and figure out the better buy. [Commercials are shown.] OK. Which store gets your business?

Sarah:	Neither. They left out too much. One car is $179 per month, and the other car is $209 per month, but they left out a lot of details.
Hannah:	I'd go to both and try to get them to compete. I'd go back and forth until one place just gave up and the other won my business.
Ms. Crawford:	Did the commercials give you enough information to do the math? Do you need to know anything more?
William:	Our family just bought a car. We asked lots of questions; those ads really don't tell you everything you need. There are trade-in questions, interest rates, and extra charges. All that tiny print on the commercial is too small to read, but you have to know what it says.
Ms. Crawford:	Good thinking. Now our brains are getting warmed-up. Let's use some of your experiences. How many of you have bought a hamburger at a fast food restaurant recently? Almost everyone, good. What did you pay for the hamburger? Let's get an answer from everyone—even if you just tell us what it costs in case you haven't actually been there recently. Any questions? Yes, Chris.
Chris:	There are lots of different burgers—plain, cheese, double-decker, bacon. Which one do you want?
Ms. Crawford:	Good point. We need to see the difference in price on the same type of product. Maybe there is something better than hamburgers. What do you think?
Chris:	How about a large soft drink at a fast food restaurant?
Ms. Crawford:	Is that better. [Heads nod yes.] OK, what is the price of a large soft drink at the fast food restaurant you've been in most recently. Let's get answers from everyone starting with Jessica.
Jessica:	$.99
Megan:	$.69
Kim:	$.69
Zach:	$.99
Tyler:	$.99
Carol:	$.89
Frances:	$.99
Matt:	$.79
Josh:	It's hard to remember. I guess $.99.
David:	$.69
Janet:	$.99
Jeremy:	$.99

Katy:	$1.29
Nathan:	I forget. Maybe $.99.
Rachel:	$.69
John:	$.99
Michelle:	$.89
Angel:	$.79
Thomas:	$.99
Jake:	$1.09
Ashley:	$.99
Mike:	$1.19
Chris:	$.99
James:	$.69
Emily:	$.79
William:	$.99
Hannah:	$.99
Sarah:	$.79
Ms. Crawford:	$.99

Ms. Crawford: OK. What can we conclude? What was the most common price? Jeremy?

Jeremy: I guess $.99 was.

Zach: Yeah, but there was a big range from $.69 to more than $1. Plus, that 2-liter bottle we talked about has more in it, but costs about the same as a large soft drink in a restaurant.

Ms. Crawford: Good thinking. Jeremy, the $.99 price was mentioned most. Zach, you are right. Maybe you'll think of that at the next restaurant you go to. OK, let's take a last look at the soft drink bottle I brought. This product is sold in stores all over town at different prices. How does a store owner or manager determine the price to charge? Of course, some large companies tell the local store manger the price that is to be charged, but even then, someone had to figure out what price to use. What facts go into determining the price a store will charge for this 2-liter bottle of soft drink?

Rachel: What the store had to pay for it.

James: All the expenses the store has.

Nathan: How many they can sell at a certain price. I'd buy lots of those for $.49, but none for $2.00 each.

Ms. Crawford: Good thinking. Those are real reasons, and there are others, but the idea seems to make sense. Any questions? No, OK, Matt, tell us what we know so far.

Matt: We know that talking about food makes you hungry. We know that the same product sells for different prices at different stores. We know that you can do the math to figure out where to shop.

Ms. Crawford: Good. Here's an example of what we'll do next. I got these numbers from the PTA president. The PTA runs the concession stand at ball games. They keep track of their sales, and they experiment with different prices. They tried selling pizza for $1.50 per slice, $1.25 per slice and $1.00 per slice. They paid $6.00 per pizza and got eight slices per pizza, so they paid how much per slice?

Emily: $.75.

Ms. Crawford: Right. Here's the chart the PTA provided to me. Everyone look at the screen, please. [The chart was prepared in advance for use on an overhead projector.]

PTA Cost	Price to Customer	Profit per Unit	Units (slices) Sold per Game	Profit
$.75	$1.50	$.75	42	$31.50
$.75	$1.25	$.50	87	$43.50
$.75	$1.00	$.25	146	$36.50

OK. Let's summarize the facts. Katy, what are the facts?

Katy: The cost to the PTA was $.75 per slice of pizza. The PTA sold pizza at different games for different prices. The lower the price they charged, the more slices of pizza they sold. The biggest profit was when they charged $1.25 per slice.

Ms. Crawford: Great summary. Any other conclusions from anyone? Yes, Frances.

Frances: Maybe the $1.00 price is good. They sold lots more pizza and maybe people got thirsty and bought more soft drinks so the PTA made money that way.

Ms. Crawford: Good thinking, Frances. That means the PTA may need to look at the total of pizza profit and soft drink profit. Also, if they sold a lot of pizza at $1.00, they might sell less candy because people got full on pizza. They really have to consider the total profit and the sales of every item. Good job. OK, now we'll move on. I'm handing out information that is like the PTA data. You will have numbers from a local business. These are real numbers provided to me by people I know at local stores. Take the information about cost, price, and profit to make a chart showing the information. Your chart will be similar to the one on the overhead. The chart will present your data and your profit calculation. Then, you'll write a one-paragraph explanation of the best price to charge based on the data in your chart. Each person will put his or her chart on the chalkboard or on computer. The seven students whose turns come up next on the computer list may use the computers today. We'll hear a 30-second presentation from each student, and we'll see if people agree with your conclusion about the best price to charge. We'll hear as many presentations today as possible. Any questions?

Jeremy: Do we use our own paper, or is there a hand-out sheet?

Ms. Crawford: Use your paper, please, to do your chart and your paragraph. This should take about 6 to 8 minutes, so let's go. You will turn in your papers with charts and paragraph today.

Note: Ms. Crawford moves from student to student during these 8 minutes. She speaks to each student rather than merely observing from above. She offers ideas via questions, "What happens if you put this column at the end?" She identifies errors, "Check that profit calculation for forty-two compact discs at $12.98 each." She encourages, "Great looking chart. Maybe you could do the next one I need for the overhead, Megan." She prevents problems or wasted time, "Tyler, Hannah, you've got 3 minutes left." She makes everyone aware of time, "You should complete your chart in 1 minute and then start your paragraph."

Ms. Crawford is not

- sitting at her desk watching the students;
- sitting at her desk grading papers, reading a book, or doing anything else;
- making a phone call in the office; or
- acting like a classroom clerk.

Examples of the data Ms. Crawford provided to students are below. Profits are shown here, but were not provided to the students; profits are to be calculated by the students.

Compact Discs:	Cost to Store	Price to Customer	Profit per Unit	Units Sold	Profit
	$6.00	$13.98	$7.98	11	$87.78
	$6.00	$12.98	$6.98	18	$125.64
	$6.00	$11.98	$5.98	22	$131.56
	$6.00	$10.98	$4.98	37	$184.26
	$6.00	$ 9.98	$3.98	52	$206.96

French Fries:	Cost to Store	Price to Customer	Profit per Unit	Units Sold	Profit
	$ .24	$ .99	$ .75	6	$ 4.50
	$ .24	$ .89	$ .65	14	$ 9.10
	$ .24	$ .79	$ .55	25	$13.75
	$ .24	$ .69	$ .45	41	$18.45
	$ .24	$ .59	$ .35	51	$17.85

T-Shirts:	Cost to Store	Price to Customer	Profit per Unit	Units Sold	Profit
	$4.95	$12.95	$8.00	21	$168.00
	$4.95	$11.95	$7.00	29	$203.00
	$4.95	$10.95	$6.00	37	$222.00
	$4.95	$ 9.95	$5.00	72	$360.00
	$4.95	$ 8.95	$4.00	82	$328.00

New Car:	Cost to Store	Price to Customer	Profit per Unit	Units Sold	Profit
	$12,400	$20,995	$8,595	3	$25,785
	$12,400	$19,895	$7,495	3	$22,485
	$12,400	$18,500	$6,100	4	$24,400
	$12,400	$17,495	$5,095	5	$25,475
	$12,400	$16,500	$4,100	6	$24,600

Ms. Crawford: OK. All the charts are finished, and everyone is completing their paragraphs. Take the next minute to wrap up the paragraphs. We'll start with the students who printed their charts from the computer. While each student gives us a summary of his or her data and conclusion, our job is to listen. When the presenter is finished, we'll ask questions, and we'll check to see if we agree with the recommended price. I did not see any math errors that went uncorrected, but if you see a calculation error, please tell us. OK. Jake, you are first.

Jake: My information was about french fries sold at a local restaurant. The restaurant spends $.24 on a serving of fries. They tried prices of $.99, $.89, $.79, $.69, and $.59. As you can see from my chart, the total profit was the highest at $.69, but they did sell more servings at $.59. Ninety-nine cents and $.89 were way too high. I'd recommend the $.69

price because the total profit was highest then, but the $.59 price could be a good sale item. Does anyone have a question?

Michelle: What do you think would happen if they set the price at $.49? That means you could get two for a dollar.

Carol: That might work. Some stores price things two for a certain amount.

Ms. Crawford: How could you use math to help you decide if two for $1.00 is a good idea? Jake?

Jake: Well. Figure the costs, price, and the profit. Try it in a restaurant, and see what happens.

Ms. Crawford: Good job, Jake. Who agrees with Jake's $.59 recommendation—hands up? All but three of you. OK. Let's keep going. James is next.

Stop. Reflect on what has happened in this math class.

- Every student has been involved.
- The teacher has directly, one-on-one interacted with each student.
- Basic math skills have been used.
- Math skills are being applied to answer real-life questions.
- The numbers being used by students are meaningful—they relate to situations that impact and interest students, such as buying a compact disc, eating at a fast-food restaurant, shopping for clothes, or buying a car.
- The work the students are doing is not a sterile, empty set of pointless problems from a textbook; rather, this work actually shows that math matters in the lives of students now.
- Each student is responsible for doing his or her work with a set of numbers that only he or she has.
- The numbers have to be completed, organized, and analyzed so a conclusion can be drawn.
- The students have to make sense of the numbers; they have to find meaning from the numbers. They must do the basic calculations, but they also must do more than calculate—they must reason, analyze, conclude, and apply.
- The teacher is constantly moving throughout the room. Much misbehavior can be prevented by great teaching that fascinates students. Students usually cooperate with teaching that fascinates them and with teachers who fascinate them.
- The class began with several short, relevant, interesting examples of numbers used by businesses. This established the topic and built a

foundation for the lesson. This also generated some interest and curiosity.

- Student input was used and, therefore, was evidence that the teacher and the students were going to work together and to learn together. Students seek people who take them seriously, who involve them, who enable them to have an impact. If these yearnings of students are included in the classroom process of learning, then students may (1) increase their commitment to school and (2) not have to look in destructive places for people who and for activities that will take them seriously, give them impact, and involve them.

Create in your mind the picture of Ms. Crawford's classroom. The walls are covered with posters, signs, advertisements, restaurant menus, and other promotional material from local businesses. The students are constantly reminded of the importance of numbers as they look throughout the classroom.

Ms. Crawford has seven computers in the room—she got five of them from a local business that recently upgraded its computer system and was glad to make the donation. The school bought the other two computers.

Ms. Crawford's chalk board is organized into twenty-one sections—seven sections on each of the three big slabs of chalkboard. Twenty-one students can put problems, charts, graphs, or calculations on the board at one time.

A bulletin board has news on it about homework, upcoming tests, math club, school events, students' birthdays, and the schedules of all school sports teams, music groups, and other performing groups.

Ms. Crawford's classroom is a fascinating place. It is vibrant, energetic, intriguing, creative, student-centered, and math-centered. The classroom is also a demanding place where Ms. Crawford is in charge. You don't mess with Ms. Crawford—she will do anything legal and proper for students to help them learn, but she will do anything legal and proper to a student who tries to interfere. Ms. Crawford prefers to team-up with students. She tells them, "If you fight me, I'll win. If you team-up with me, everyone wins."

Back to the lesson. After Jake's presentation, each student will make a presentation. This may take the class into a second day—that is fine because Ms. Crawford knows the importance of each student learning how to speak effectively to a group. Each presentation includes some questions from students and from Ms. Crawford. This interaction can be used to cause important learning and is, therefore, a good use of time. After the final presentation, Ms. Crawford will lead a discussion of overall ideas that emerged from the content and the conclusions of each student.

Ms. Crawford:　Great work, all of you. Now we know how you would price each product you worked on and heard about. Let's look for some common ideas that applied to several or most of the charts. For example, was the highest price to the customer always the worst or the best price to charge? Think. Now, while you think about those topics, we have a bonus. Remember we discussed the PTA pizza prices? Well, two PTA members are coming to our room now to serve pizza to you. I told them you were great students and that we were working on a math project that included price calculations, so they are donating pizzas. Ms. Thomas, Mr. Jenkins, thanks for coming here to give pizza to these scholars. Now, while you eat, you have to think. Tell us the big ideas that emerged from hearing all the presentations and seeing all the charts. Yes, Katy.

Katy: Usually a lower price increased sales enough to increase the profit, but sometimes the unit profit went too low and the sales increase did not make up the difference. So, lower seemed to be better, but, well, not always best.

Ms. Crawford: Super answer. You expressed a very big idea in a very clear way. What else Janet, what do you think?

Janet: I've heard people say that if something costs a lot it must be a better product. I guess that is true sometimes, like a Mercedes car, but you have to shop around.

Ms. Crawford: So, the high price may be worth it, but you have to check it out, right?

Megan: Right, plus, some prices are marked down to get rid of junk. Then, the price on new stuff goes back up. I guess stores have to be ready to change prices when it is necessary. That's my conclusion. There may not be one price that is perfect forever.

Ms. Crawford: Good thinking. Let's get one more big idea.

David: I saw a big idea. This was pretty easy to do. I thought that figuring out prices would be super complicated, but if you do the math right and think, it's not so hard.

Ms. Crawford: Wonderful point. All of you did the math. All of you explained the pricing well. Sure, every student in here could help a business determine proper pricing because you can do the math and you can think. Now, let's apply this to school. Think of two numbers that we could chart at school. For example, a basketball coach could chart free throws made and games won to see how important free throws are to winning. We could chart your attendance at school and your grades to see how those are related. What else could we chart at school?

Tyler:	I know. The days they serve pizza in the cafeteria and the number of students who buy lunch in the cafeteria. Pizza days get more customers, I bet.
Kim:	The number of boys who get suspended from school and the number of girls who get suspended.
Ms. Crawford:	What could you relate the suspensions to? I can tell you that more boys are suspended than girls, but how about everyone who gets suspended charted with their grades? That might reveal something.
Kim:	How about people who get suspended and their grades last year? Maybe we could predict.
Ms. Crawford:	Wow. What an idea. OK. Keep going. Josh?
Josh:	I really don't know.
Ms. Crawford:	Well, think. What did you hear many students say?
Josh:	That the PTA pizza we ate was good.
Ms. Crawford:	You're right. It was good. Would you pay $1.25 per slice for it at a game?
Josh:	No.
Ms. Crawford:	How much would you pay?
Josh:	I know they pay $.75 per slice, so I'd offer them $.75, take it or leave it.
Ms. Crawford:	So your big idea is that businesses should price for no profit. They'd go broke.
Josh:	Whatever.
Ms. Crawford:	Who knows why the PTA can't charge $.75 per slice?
Jessica:	They have to make money. They aren't selling pizza just so we get fed for a low price. They are making money for the school.
Ms. Crawford:	Good point. What Josh and Jessica have said supports this idea—do the math. Zero profit equals no business.

Note: Josh was not interested in class, and he attempted to disrupt the class with his comical comment. Ms. Crawford still used what Josh said as a basis for her next questions and as a way to make a point. Josh did not intend to cooperate, but Ms. Crawford took Josh's comment and with some theatrical license used that comment when she said, "What Josh and Jessica have said supports this idea—do the math." Did Josh's comments really support the idea of do the math? No, not as Josh stated his comments, but yes as Ms. Crawford quickly applied Josh's comment in a constructive way. Now Josh is sitting in class wondering (1) I must be smarter than I thought (2) I guess I showed Ms. Crawford that I know my stuff or (3) did she just say that my idea was important? How did that happen? What's going on here?

Ms. Crawford: OK. We began this lesson with numbers that businesses used in prices that were communicated through newspaper ads, television ads, and other ways. We considered prices from places where we have shopped. The prices are chosen for reasons, and we explored the impact of different numbers, actually different prices, being selected. You calculated the unit profit and the total profit from the example you were given, and you analyzed the numbers to select the best price. We've heard your presentations, we've put some big ideas together, and we've applied the process of analyzing numbers to some situations at school. I have the paragraphs you wrote. I'll read them tonight and return them to you tomorrow so you'll know your grade on the paragraph and on the presentation you made in class. Any questions at this point? No? OK. Who knows what our topic is for tomorrow? It is on the weekly schedule you copied on Monday.

Angel: It says graphing.

Ms. Crawford: Right. You took numbers and made a chart. Another way to present those numbers is on a graph. The idea is to show the relationship between numbers, how the numbers impact each other.

John: Hey, Carol, you know a lot about relationships, don't you? Do you have a boyfriend graph?

Ms. Crawford: Carol, it's not worth it. Please keep cool. I owe you one if you ignore him, OK? Now, John, your comment was wrong. I'll see you after class about that. What you don't realize is that the word *relationship* applies in math with numbers just as it does if life with people. In 20 seconds, the number on the clock in the office changes and that causes a bell to ring. What will all of you do then? John, what will the students do?

John: Get up, I guess.

Ms. Crawford: Right, the students will get up and go to their next class. There is a relationship between time and actions. OK, tomorrow we work on graphs and graphing. We got a lot done today—good job. See you tomorrow.

Note: Two seconds after Ms. Crawford said "tomorrow," the bell rang. She always manages her classes to avoid wasting time. She spoke with John about his improper comment and explained to him that her actions would include a reduction in his classroom conduct grade and a phone call to his family and that at the end of class tomorrow, John would apologize to the class for being disruptive. He would have the rest of the day to apologize personally to Carol. If that was not done, the incident would be handled by a school counselor or administrator. John needs to know that every student deserves to be free from insults and that the classroom is a place of work and responsibility, not of play and nonsense.

Ms. Crawford spent a few seconds during class on this matter, but she did not lose stride with teaching. She took John's misuse of the word *relationship* and emphasized the point about numbers relating to each other. Ms. Crawford cannot control everything that happens in her classroom, but she can control her reaction to everything that happens in her classroom. She could let small problems totally destroy her work, but she has learned to turn small problems into large opportunities. She is the adult. She is the teacher. She is in charge. She will cause learning even if an unexpected situation occurs.

REFLECTING ON THE CLASSROOM VISIT

Read the following question, please, then set this book down and think: "If I were a student in Ms. Crawford's classroom, what would I remember about the class on numbers, charts, prices, and profit?

Now, list what students could remember:

(1) Eating PTA pizza in class

(2) Doing the math

(3) Watching TV commercials

(4) The newspaper ads

(5) Discussing prices from different stores

(6) The presentations students made

(7) Calculating unit profit and total profit

(8) Organizing data in a chart

(9) Determining the best price

(10) Writing a paragraph

(11) John insulting Carol

(12) Applying the chart idea to situations at school

(13)

(14)

(15)

(16)

(17)

If Ms. Crawford had used the lesson plan briefly mentioned on page 111: "Read pages 46 and 47. We'll go over some examples. You'll do a worksheet, and then you have odd-numbered problems 1–15 for homework," what would students remember?

(1)

(2)

(3)

(4)

(5)

The author cannot identify many aspects of the boring class that are worth remembering. People remember interaction. People forget worksheets, odd-numbered problems, and classroom activities that pass time or cover material. Ms. Crawford's class caused learning through constant intellectual, instructional, and human interaction. There was an intensity that was created in Ms. Crawford's classroom as one teacher and twenty-eight students encountered many ideas, moved at a compelling pace, used skills, and probed for meaning.

What reason would be given for (a) not planning lessons as Ms. Crawford did and for (b) not teaching as Ms. Crawford does?

(1) Time

(2) I'm just not like Ms. Crawford—different teachers teach different ways.

Time

Let's do the math:

	365	days per year
−	190	days teachers are at school with students or for meetings, professional development, record keeping, or other duties
=	175	days teachers are not in school
−	104	total days per year in weekends
=	71	non-school days, non-weekend days; Mondays through Fridays that teachers are not in school or 14 weeks of Monday through Friday.

It is simply not accurate and not honest for a teacher to use the excuse, "I don't have time to plan fascinating, interactive lessons."

Teachers are paid a full-time salary, but work 38 weeks per year. Teachers are off for Christmas/winter beak, for Easter/spring break, for many days throughout the school year—such as Labor Day, Thanksgiving, Martin Luther King Jr. Day, President's Day, Memorial Day, and others according to local customs—and for summer vacation.

Some teachers conscientiously use the time away from school to earn a graduate degree, to attend useful conferences or workshops, to volunteer time, or to prepare their materials and lessons for upcoming classes. Other teachers take second or third jobs and if their family budget requires this, that is understandable, but that does not excuse those teachers from being responsible for causing learning. If teaching does not pay enough for a person to meet financial obligations, there are options, such as (a) sponsoring a school club or team and receiving extra pay for that, (b) asking the administrators in your school district about additional duties, perhaps to rewrite a curriculum, for extra pay, (c) reviewing your personal budget to see if some expenses could be reduced so the second or third job could be eliminated, (d) changing jobs altogether—teachers know what their salary is going to be prior to signing a contract. If the salary is not sufficient for you, do not teach.

Different Teachers Teach in Different Ways

Imagine a student giving this explanation for why his or her homework—a five-page report on an important inventor—is being handed in 3 days late, four pages short, and is about an athlete instead of an inventor: "Different students do homework in different ways." The teacher would give the student an F and may take action about the defiant attitude.

Under the concept of "academic freedom," the education profession has protected the professional discretion of teachers to do in their classrooms what they think is right or what they can otherwise defend. Despite this sometimes being an excuse for teachers just doing what they have always done or for teachers doing what is easy, the education profession has been reluctant to require that teachers change their methods even when the results of existing methods were unacceptable.

The excuse, "Well, that's just not how I teach," is invalid. The duty of a teacher is to cause learning; therefore, the methods used by a conscientious teacher are those that cause the most learning and the best learning, not those that the teacher learned years ago, is comfortable with, and has already made copies of for all the classes he or she will teach from now until retirement. Yes, there are many effective ways to teach so that learning is caused; however, teachers who use methods that do not cause learning must change their methods. Teachers should be free to select from all effective teaching methods, not from all methods.

This book includes the forms—the Basic Concept, the Instruction Grid, and the six-part sequence—that teachers can use to help design fascinating, three-dimensional lessons that have intellectual intensity and instructional intensity. Those forms can help teachers plan efficiently and effectively. Use those forms repeatedly, and interactive lessons can become a habit.

HUMAN RESOURCES

There is another resource that teachers use far too rarely—each other. The education profession has created a level of comfortable isolation. This teacher mentality could be described as "I go in my classroom, close the door, teach my students, and go home at the end of the day." This perspective assumes that education is compartmentalized into daily portions as students move from class to class, teacher to teacher. Do this for 13 years, and you get a high school diploma.

Wait. Education is interactive. Spelling interacts with reading. Math interacts with science. History interacts with foreign languages. If we expect students to realize the connections between all subjects and all learning, then the teachers of all subjects need to connect with each other.

The author has worked for three large companies. In each company, the employees constantly interacted with each other. Everyone had individual duties, but everyone also shared comprehensive responsibilities. No single employee could do his or her job without productive interaction with other workers. This perspective says that the company's product must be great for my part of the product to be seen as great and vice versa.

In education, that perspective would be translated, "Every student at our school learns or every employee at our school needs to do more and/or better work." But, the reader says, how can I help a student who is not in my class? By working together with colleagues so everyone in the school knows the best ideas that everyone else has about teaching.

When would the teachers have these conversations, these shared planning sessions? What happens if teachers return to school a week early in August/September and create lessons together? What happens if teachers stay after school 1 hour each week to plan lessons together? What happens if some days that school districts allocate to professional development become days of professionals working together at their school for their students?

Who would pay the teachers for any extra days or hours of working together? There would be no extra pay. Until every student learns—and that is not the case currently—what justification is there for higher pay? The duty of a teacher is to cause learning; therefore, do what it takes to complete that duty without expecting extra pay.

In this chapter, a script of a class was presented. Many readers may have responded to that script, "I could do that." Of course, you can. Fascinating teaching is not a skill available only to that rare master of the classroom. Every teacher can do what fascinating teachers do.

This chapter also reviewed the process for planning fascinating lessons. Two resources are easily available—the forms in this book and other teachers.

EVALUATING STUDENTS

Now, with new awareness of how to plan a fascinating lesson and how to implement a fascinating lesson, it is reasonable to review how students will be tested or assessed. The old worksheet system was its own testing method. The student filled in the blanks correctly or did not. How will students in fascinating classrooms be evaluated? They will be evaluated by their performance on each portion of the lesson.

How did Ms. Crawford evaluate her students? She graded their paragraphs about the best price and she graded their presentations in class. The paragraph and the presentation would be judged against the class rubric, which clearly describes the levels of work that could exist. The rubric she used is below and was shared with students in advance of their work so they know the standards:

- Fascinating (Grade A): The student accurately completes all calculations and shows all work. Work is perfectly organized and legible. There are no writing errors. The student presents compelling ideas with convincing reasons and rationale. The student extends the assigned tasks via application to a relevant part of his or her life. The student gives evidence of mastering the basic skills of the task and of using those skills in meaningful ways.
- Interesting (Grade B or C): The student completes all or almost all calculations and shows all or almost all work. Work is organized and can be understood, but some improvement was possible. There were a few writing errors. Ideas are supported, but some reasoning or conclusions could be stronger. The assigned tasks are applied, but not really beyond the assigned topic. Basic skills are handled, with some possible improvement. Use of the basic skills is starting to move toward meaningful ways.
- Not Good Enough (Grade D or F and must be done over): The student completes some or none of the assigned work. Organization is weak or missing altogether. Several or many errors in calculations and in writing were made. Conclusions are vague or wrong. Rationale is not convincing or is simply wrong. Little or no application beyond the task was made. Basic skills are not mastered. The work shows no effort to construct meaning.

The rubric has helped students realize that quantity and quality are expected. A successful student must do all that is required and must do all of that well. The rubric works for the variety of assignments that Ms. Crawford uses, including those which follow. Please note, there are times when Ms. Crawford is testing to confirm that students have mastered precise skills or have mentally acquired exact information. A student may get a score of 92%

on a test that had fifty math problems with forty-six done correctly; however, it is rare that Ms. Crawford's tests are *only* testing for acquisition of information or for mastery of a precise, basic skill. Even with a test of fifty math problems, Ms. Crawford usually includes one or two writing questions so the students apply the basic skills in a meaningful, challenging, and intellectually intense way. Ms. Crawford and similar teachers use many methods to assess students including the following:

(1) Presentation in class

(2) Writing assignment

(3) A poster or other graphic creation

(4) Math problems

(5) Inventing a new product that uses numbers

(6) Report on how math is used by people in various jobs

(7) Analysis of statistics to emphasize conclusions

(8) Putting a math problem on the chalkboard

(9) Bringing to class a newspaper story that relied on numbers to make its point

(10) Create a song, skit, or commercial about a concept in math

(11) More math problems (the basics are essential)

(12) A project that combines math with another class done in cooperation with other teachers

(13)

(14)

(15)

(16)

(17)

(Please add ideas to complete the list.)

The word *authentic* is used to describe assessment of students when the emphasis is on both knowing and applying. The idea is that if students do nothing but hear the teacher, read the textbook, complete the worksheet, and take a test that measures the student's memory of what the teacher said, what the textbook authors wrote, and what the worksheet author left as a blank to fill in, those students were assessed in an inauthentic way, a way that is used only in school and has no meaning, purpose, or use other than to show that material was covered and papers were graded.

Some information does have to be memorized. Some teacher words must be recalled verbatim. Some textbooks have ideas worth remembering. There may even be a worksheet that is worth using! Teachers cannot dismiss these sources as inauthentic, so let's use the word *meaningful* to describe the way that students are tested, assessed, or evaluated in fascinating classrooms.

The assessment itself should be a teaching method. It should reveal to the student some result that has meaning. The rubric presented earlier does that by helping the student understand what was done well and what must be done over. It is meaningful because it is interactive. The teacher does more than put a letter grade on the paper. The teacher writes sentences on the paper so the student understands how and why his or her work measured up to the standard of the rubric.

APPLICATION OF INFORMATION

This chapter concludes with a story about a student. The next chapter will go further into the step-by-step process of implementing fascinating teaching in a classroom and in a school by presenting a plan for teacher training.

Mom and Brian had made a deal. He could go to a week of basketball camp in July if he first attended a week of teen leadership camp in June. The leadership camp was actually outdoor camping; and if the weather was good, the week might be tolerable. Basketball camp would be at a university, and living in the dorm would be nothing but fun. Brian accepted the deal, and Mom accepted the fact that her son would put lots more effort into week of basketball than into a week of leadership camp.

When she picked Brian up at the end of leadership camp, Mom asked the typical questions that any adult would ask, "Well, what did you learn?"

Brian gave the typical teenager's answer, "Oh, some stuff about people and how to get along and how to stay away from everything that is bad for you. We played some games, and we cooked out every meal. It wasn't too bad."

Mom pressed a bit further. "Brian, tell me one specific lesson that you learned."

"Easy. Our camp director said that we had to respect the property of the camp and of each person. He said it was like what people were told thousands of year ago, 'You shall not steal.' So I learned that a long time ago people were told not to steal. I even memorized the rule—you shall not steal."

"Good. Now, don't we need to go get some new basketball shoes for you so you'll be ready for that camp?"

"Great idea, Mom. Thanks."

The basketball camp attracted more than 400 players. Brian saw some friends from school at the camp registration. The days were packed with drills, instruction, games, and films. There were lots of demonstrations, lots of work on game situations, hundreds of pick-up games, and endless sprints to run. Camp was good.

Mom picked up Brian when camp was over. Actually, Mom went to the closing ceremony at camp when awards were given out and when the final four teams from the camp tournament had their championship. Trophies, t-shirts, and basketballs were given to the players on those four teams.

"OK, Brian. What did you learn at camp?" Mom asked the standard question on the way home.

"Mom, it was so cool. We learned everything. We worked on free throws, three-point shots, defense, offense, rebounding, full-court pressure, and other stuff. We played on teams. We played one-on-one and three-on-three. We did it all. I really know a lot about basketball now. I think I can make the team at school."

When they got home, Mom and Brian each had chores to do. The grass needed to be cut, and that was Brian's duty. Supper needed to be fixed, and Mom would be in charge of that. Dad would be home soon. He and Mom owned a florist shop, and it had been his day to close the store.

"Hey, Brian, how was camp?" Dad asked as he got out of his car as Brian was putting the lawn mower away.

"It was great, Dad. Think you can keep up with me in a game of one-on-one?"

Dad answered as they walked into the house and joined Mom in the kitchen. "Sure son. We'll play tonight. I need to find my basketball shoes. I was looking for them a couple of days ago when I wanted to play tennis. Has anyone see them?"

"Oh, yeah, Dad. I have them. I took them to camp in case I needed an extra pair. You know, I was still getting used to the new shoes Mom got me."

"Did you ask me first, Brian, or did you just take them?" Dad asked with some frustration.

"Uh, well, you know, I just figured it was OK. I'm sorry."

"Brian, I actually did need those shoes a few days ago. It would be better if you had asked to borrow them."

Mom took this moment to make a point. "Brian, remember what you told me you memorized at the teen leadership camp?"

"Mom, that was weeks ago. How can you expect me to always remember that? This is different. Be fair. Dad is getting his shoes back."

"Brian, what did you memorize?"

"I memorized some little saying from thousands of years ago. It was for people a long time ago. Things are different now."

Mom waited a moment before speaking. "Brian, what you memorized was supposed to be put to use. You remember the words, don't you?"

"Yes, Mom. You shall not steal."

"OK, Brian. That is not just a rule for people a few thousand years ago. It is a rule now. You've memorized the words, but you also have to understand the idea—you don't take anything that does not belong to you, even if it is like your father's shoes and you think he won't mind. You have to think about what you memorized, and you need to apply what you memorized so it helps you to live a better life."

It was Dad's turn. "Brian, when we play basketball after supper you'll apply all the new basketball skills you learned at camp. You did not memorize those skills only to keep them in your memory. You practiced them at camp, you thought about them, and you really understood what the coaches were trying to get you to do. Now you are ready to apply those skills in a game with me. Get it, son?"

"Yes, sir. I get it. Am I in trouble?"

"Well, yes, but you can work your way out of trouble. Before we play basketball, you do all of the kitchen cleaning after supper, but first go get my shoes. I'm going to practice basketball while you clean the dishes. I'll need the extra help to keep up with you. Plus, you know our rule—you will write an essay about how you could have handled this situation better."

Supper was good. Mom fixed lasagna, which is Brian's favorite. That meal does make for some dirty dishes, so Brian had lots of kitchen work to do. The basketball game with Dad actually became the best two out of three. Brian won, but the games were very close, and the last one went into overtime because you had to win by two.

Brian spent some time writing his essay that night. His writing included a strong conclusion:

"So if I take what I memorized at leadership camp and use it the way I am using what I learned at basketball camp, I'll be a better person. I memorized the words, but I really did not think about what they mean. I obviously did not understand them, or I would have realized that I needed to ask my father before I used his basketball shoes. Memorizing the words did not mean I really understood the words or that I would apply those words. I need to do that. I did not want to write this, but I had to, and it was my fault."

CHAPTER 6

Implementation Via Professional Development

School administrators work with teachers whose skills, motivation, work ethic, and effectiveness vary. What is a principal to do to help each teacher cause learning despite the range in ability and commitment? This chapter shows some ways that methods in this book can be taught to teachers.

Some teachers went to college, learned a way of teaching, and made a career of 30 years by doing nothing more and nothing less than what they learned to do in college. Their levels of effectiveness varied, but may have skewed low as their methods lost impact.

Some other teachers discard all materials each year and begin anew to create the best lessons possible using some of what has worked before, but always seeking better ideas, methods, and experiences to share with students. They get results.

Some teachers are convinced that their duty is limited to giving students the opportunity to learn. These teachers often rely on textbooks and worksheets. They work 8 hours daily and rarely have inspired, encouraged, amazed, or fascinated a student. Their level of effectiveness vary, but skews low.

Other teachers accept that their duty is to cause learning. These good people constantly demand the best of themselves and simultaneously inspire the best from their students. These teachers fascinate students. They get results.

What is known by the fascinated and fascinating teachers can be taught to other current teachers and to all future teachers. This chapter presents a professional development plan that could be used with a faculty, in a department, by teachers on a grade level or by an individual teacher.

PROFESSIONAL development, teacher in-service, or teacher training by any name is often evaluated by teachers as classroom experiences are often evaluated by students: Boring. Criticism this author has had throughout his career toward professional development is, "OK, I've heard your lecture, now

133

what do I do in my classroom tomorrow that will make me a better teacher and that will make my students better students?" Few professional development presentations or teacher training programs the author has attended were relevant, challenging, meaningful, intense, or fascinating. The question "Why are we attending this training?" has always been answered by a colleague who said, "Keen, we're just putting in hours." That is similar to bored students who are just putting in years until graduation.

Professional development sessions typically involve a guest speaker or a visiting presenter who knows little or nothing about the school he or she is visiting, but who does know, claim to know, or pretend to know something that someone decided a faculty or administrator group needed to hear. Ten minutes into the presentation, many audience members have given up any optimism and are counting the minutes until lunch. A few people pay attention, others do paperwork, some whisper to each other, and a few sleep. These adults are absolutely bored.

PROFESSIONAL DEVELOPMENT FOR A GROUP

Warm-up

To implement fascinating teaching using a different approach to professional development begins with asking, "What would a student tell teachers about fascinating teaching?" If we asked Jared, Heather, and Owen to show teachers what fascinates them, where would they take their teachers? Perhaps to karate class, theater class, and guitar/band practice. The professional development suggested here begins with going to watch children and teenagers do what fascinates them, plus participating in the activity that fascinated the students.

Imagine that on August 15 the faculty of a school is going to be trained in the process of three-dimensional teaching using the Interaction Lesson Plan—Basic Concept, Instruction Grid, and six-part sequence in this book. During the week of August 8–14, each member of the faculty will conduct some research individually or with a colleague. The research will be a combination of anthropology, sociology, and psychology. The goals are to (1) observe children and young people doing something that fascinates them and (2) to participate in the activity so that the observer now experiences fascination.

For example, I have a neighbor who has a trampoline. Local children spend hours in pure fascination as they play on the trampoline. Their conversation is constant. They invent games and contests. They imitate each other. They interact with each other, with the trampoline, and with the experience of trampolining. Watching them offers insight into what fascinates these children. Joining them in a trampoline session could provide deeper understanding as one could capture the feeling, the process, and the results of total fascination.

So, during August 8–14, the faculty members have research to do. Where should they go?

(1) A skateboard or rollerblade park

(2) A videogame arcade

(3) Little league baseball practice

(4) A school sports team practice

(5) A dance for teenagers

(6) A skating rink

(7) A shopping mall

(8) A bowling alley

(9) The local restaurant hang-out

(10) Summer camp

(11) A church youth group social event or Bible study

(12) A carnival or fair

(13) A concert with music teenagers like

(14) A circus

(15) A music shop

(16) A college or university campus

(17) Karate class

(18) A private music lesson

(19) A restaurant that caters to children

(20) A toy store

(21) A museum for children

(22) A weekend movie, to watch a film that is purely for teenagers or children

(23) A bookstore for children

(24) A video rental store

(25) A restaurant where many teenagers work

(26) A high-school sporting event or practice

(27) An orientation program for new students at a school other than where you teach

(28) A teenage nightclub

(29) A high-school marching band practice

(30) A swimming pool

(31) An amusement park

(32) A professional sports event

(33) In the yard, in the basement, or in a park to watch children invent a game

(34) A birthday party

(35) Playing with toys or games at their homes

(36)

(37)

(38)

(39)

(40)

(Please complete the list with items 36 through 40.)

The professional development program on August 15 will begin with . . . food! Let the teachers know that their hunger will be taken care of and that they will be pampered.

Drills

Next, each teacher is given a one-page summary of the game of checkers. The summary has the rules, the information needed to begin play, and some ideas about how to win. Then, teachers will pair up and play checkers. After that, everyone goes to the computer lab to play checkers on the computer.

Observers will hear comments such as, "I haven't played checkers for years," "that was fun," or "I had no idea you could play checkers on the computer."

When the teachers return from the computer lab to where the meeting is being held, discuss the difference in the experiences of reading about checkers, playing the game using a checker board, and playing checkers on a computer. Probe for the factors that made playing checkers interesting and even fascinating.

Notice that when people play checkers, they talk to each other. They naturally interact.

Now, everyone goes into the gym where volleyball nets are set up. Divide into four teams, and play volleyball according to the proper rules of the game. Then make one change—the object of the game no longer is to prevent the other team from returning the ball. The object is to see how many times the two teams on opposite sides of the net can return the ball to each other. After a few minutes, ask people what changed in their thinking and in their actions when the object of the game changed.

It's time to return to the meeting room. "The big idea for today is to change the object of teaching from teachers versus students or students versus teachers so we will make school, classes, and learning so fascinating that everyone teams up, teachers and students. Sure, it is idealistic, but unless and until we all move in the same direction, our results will be limited."

Note: Another game could substitute for checkers or another activity altogether could substitute for the checkers activity as long as the key points are made:

(1) Playing checkers is much more likely to fascinate someone than reading about checkers is, but you must learn the rules before you play. The basics are essential!

(2) The computer did not change the game, but added a screen with graphics and perhaps with sound. For some teachers, this may be an awakening about how interesting computer interaction can be.

(3) People talk, interact, and compete when they play checkers. This just happens and is part of what children or teenagers do as they play any game or share any adventure. This natural inclination to interact could be a productive part of a fascinating classroom but rarely happens in the "worksheet and questions at the end of the chapter" classroom.

Also, the volleyball activity can be replaced if another one can be used to make people think outside of their typical, habitual thinking pattern, such as work in groups to identify fifty uses of a penny.

Now, each teacher or each pair of teachers will report on their research. Where did they go? What did they see? What seemed to cause the children or teenagers to be interested in or fascinated in the activity? What do the young people look like when they are completely involved in the activity—their expression, their words, their tone, their reactions to each other? Did some young people avoid getting involved? Why?

It is helpful if the teachers are given a format in advance so as they observe they can make recordings in the topical categories that are most helpful for their presentations. The form that follows could be used:

Teacher(s) doing observation: • _____
_____

Place of observation: • _____
Date(s), time(s) of observation: • _____
Overall description of the place, setting: • _____
Age range of children and/or teenagers   • _____
  observed: _____
Narrative, including quotes, of   • _____
  observation: _____
_____

What are the young people doing?   • _____

_____

Describe how the young people look,   • _____
    sound, and act:

_____

What seems to most interest or fascinate   • _____
    the young people here?

_____

Describe your participation: • _____

_____

_____

List every possible reason for why the young people are interested in and fascinated by this place, the activities here, the people here, and their experiences here:

(1)   *(6)*
(2)   *(7)*
(3)   *(8)*
(4)   *(9)*
(5)   *(10)*

Now, what is happening at this place with/for/between/among/to/in the minds of these young people. Put yourself in their minds, and describe their thoughts, motives, goals, actions, and reactions. For example, what is that 13-year-old thinking as he bats in a little league game, or what is the 16-year-old trying to accomplish as she talks to friends at a fast food restaurant?

(1)   *(6)*
(2)   *(7)*
(3)   *(8)*
(4)   *(9)*
(5)   *(10)*

Each teacher or pair of teachers will report to the faculty in a 2- to 4-minute presentation of their findings. The report needs to convey the information in the form above, but also needs to convey the feeling/atmosphere/mood of the place and of the interaction between the children or teenagers. Teachers need to know in advance that they will be making these presentations so they can bring any props, pictures, or other items from their observations that would help their colleagues fully understand the experience that the young people had at the place that was observed.

Skills

After all presentations are made, solicit specific answers to this question: "What happened in these observed settings that caused the children or teenagers to be so interested in, excited about, concerned about, committed to, involved in, and fascinated with what they were doing?" Have people record the responses on many large, poster-size sheets of paper.

There should be dozens of answers to the questions, such as "They were with their friends," "They noticed each other," "They took each other seriously," "They listened to each other," "They laughed," "It was exciting," "They moved around," "They could win," "People cheered for them," "It just seemed really important to them," or "It was real life to them." If teachers say that some of the children or teenagers they observed were *not* involved or interested, ask what could have been done to improve that.

Now, divide the faculty into groups of four to six teachers. Give a sheet of the poster-size paper with the recorded answers to each group of teachers. The instructions are as follows: "For each statement on the sheet of paper you have, think of two ways a teacher could implement that in the classroom. For example, someone said that the students seemed fascinated because what they were doing seemed really important to them. Good. Now, create two specific actions a teacher could take so what occurs in the classroom seems really important to the students."

Set a time limit for this task so people get started and get finished on sched ule. Have a report from each group, but consider making the report more than "Our group came up with these ideas." Perhaps each group presents their ideas as a skit that resembles one of the places that had been observed. For example, the report could be given by teachers who played the roles of teenagers at the mall. Another group gives their report as if they were nine-year-olds at a birthday party.

Another way to put some energy and interest in reports is to have each group select a television program and present their report as if they are the characters in an episode of the program. Be creative—the reports could be boring or could be fascinating. Why settle for ordinary when greatness is possible?

Scrimmage

The rest of this professional development training session will concentrate on the actual planning of real lessons that teachers can use at school. Teachers will work with two or three colleagues to plan a lesson. They will use the three-dimensional process that is on pages 75–82, but that is reprinted below. It may be helpful for teachers at the same grade level to work together or for teachers of the same subject matter to work together.

"Now that we have opened our minds to some creative ideas and now that we have probed some experiences that fascinate our students in parts of their lives away from school, our adventure becomes creating lessons that we implement in our classrooms to fascinate our students. Many of the activities that you observed could be applied in your classroom. Some of the interaction between students whom you observed could be put to use in your classroom."

"Keep this in mind, please. Our students are real people who are living real lives. They do have some part of their lives that they do get very excited about, interested in, concerned about, committed to, fascinated with and successful in. For too many students, school is not a part of their life that fascinates them. All of us are convinced that education is important. We know that the students need to learn everything in our curriculum, but they often see school as boring, irrelevant, and meaningless. Still, these people do find other parts of their lives to be fascinating. No, school cannot be a party or an amusement park, and school is not fun, fun, fun; however, let's use every resource available to us to fascinate our students."

Teachers would now divide into small groups of three or four people and completely plan a three-dimensional lesson. This will probably take about 30 minutes, but the leader of the professional development can monitor to see if less time is adequate or if more time is needed. Each group will make a 2- to 4-minute presentation of their lesson, and the presentation cannot just be "our group did. . . ." This 2- to 4-minute presentation should be for the full lesson what a preview of an upcoming film is in a movie theater. The result of the presentation should be an audience that says, "Wow, I need to see that lesson!"

Creating Three-Dimensional Teaching

	How to Organize
1ST DIMENSION: A variety of purposefully planned activities.	Use the Interaction Lesson Plan—Basic Concept (see pages 30–31): 1. The purpose of this lesson is to cause learning: a. Of this idea: _____ _____ _____ b. Through these activities: _____ _____ _____ c. With this interaction _____ d. Learning will be measured by and confirmed by this method: _____ _____ _____

2ND DIMENSION:
The activities are
meaningful, ener-
getic, and dramatic.

AND

3RD DIMENSION:
Use interaction to
inform, amaze,
exercise, apply, and
challenge the mind
of each student.

This is the teacher's reality check. Fascination requires interaction. It is through student, teacher, idea, and activity interacting that depth of meaning, knowing, probing, wondering, and learning can occur and through that fascination can be ignited. The reality check to confirm that genuine, impactful interaction is occurring is the Interaction Lesson Plan—Instruction Grid.

This thirty-two-cell grid (Figure 6.1) helps guide creation of or selection of activities and the methods of interacting.

Cool-Down

The 2- to 4-minute "previews" are presented, followed by some time to discuss any common elements that were used by several groups. This may help

	Teacher Skills			
	A Challenge Students	**B** Variety of Teaching Methods	**C** Enthusiasm & Encourage- ment	**D** Connect Learning with Living
Student Skills				
1. Basics				
2. Communication				
3. Computer Use				
4. Thinking				
5. Problem Solving				
6. Life-long Learning				
7. People Skills				
8. Work Ethic				

Figure 6.1. *Thirty-Two Cell Interaction Lesson Plan—Instruction Grid.*

some teachers more specifically identify elements of instructional intensity, intellectual intensity, three-dimensional teaching, fascination in the classroom, and teaching to cause learning. It is also helpful to identify an idea, method, or technique that only one group used, but that other people could apply in their classrooms. Remember, teachers too rarely take the time, make the time, or create the opportunity to trade ideas or to work together. The comfortable isolation that some teachers seek or accept denies them the benefits of meaningful interaction with colleagues.

Huddle

The next step in the professional development training is for each teacher to individually design a three-dimensional lesson. Prior to starting their work, several teachers need to volunteer to actually present one of the lessons that has been created by the groups of teachers. While every other teacher is individually designing a three-dimensional lesson, a few teachers will go to rooms and prepare to actually teach a lesson to their colleagues. The sequence of events from this point on is as follows:

(1) All teachers individually design a three-dimensional lesson except for a few—about one out of every fifteen to twenty teachers—prepare to actually teach a lesson that was just created and "previewed" by the groups of teachers. Fifteen to 30 minutes will be needed for this.

(2) The teachers who will present a lesson are joined by fifteen to twenty colleagues. Each group of teachers will actually participate in the lesson as if they were students (please avoid the temptation to imitate only the worst student behavior; rather, be cooperative, genuine, and in keeping with the goal of learning).

(3) Each teacher who individually designed a three-dimensional lesson gives that to the people leading the training prior to going to the classrooms for the demonstration lesson. Some of the trainers and/or people at the school assisting the training will review the lesson plans while the teachers are in the demonstration lesson. The reviewed lesson will be returned before adjourning. Other trainers and/or people assisting will be in the demonstration lessons to help lead a post-lesson discussion of the lesson.

(4) Everyone returns to the main meeting room to offer thoughts, ideas, questions, problems, or comments based on the demonstration lessons. The concluding activity is for each teacher to write a letter. The letter is from a student whom the teacher will teach in the upcoming school year or is teaching now. The start of the letter is provided below. Tell the teachers to assume that the student had a great experience in their class-

room because the teacher created fascinating experiences that caused learning.

Dear _____ (teacher's name),

Well, I never thought I'd write a note to a teacher. I write notes to friends, but not to teachers.

Anyway, this year in your class was really different. It was cool. I never liked school before. I just came because I had to, but I never did much.

I had heard about you before the school year started. Bad news. Everything I heard was, I'm sorry, bad. But something changed. This was really a cool class. I thought you'd like to know what a student thinks of your teaching, so here's my review. I'm writing this like those people on TV who review movies.

Now, the task ahead of each teacher here is to do the work that results in a student having such meaningful experiences in a classroom that such a letter would be written genuinely.

PROFESSIONAL DEVELOPMENT FOR AN INDIVIDUAL

Self-Teaching

The professional development training course presented in this chapter can be modified for use by an individual teacher. The procedures below could be followed in a self-directed study.

(1) Visit several places where students who are the age of your students can be found. See the list on pages 135–136 for ideas. Observe these children or teenagers with an emphasis on their interaction, their energy level, their creativity, their comments, what they create, how they resolve disputes, what seems to most interest and fascinate them, and how they respond to the activity and to each other. If possible, participate with them—for example, if you are at an amusement park, get on the rides, even those you prefer to avoid, and try to capture the same experience that the children or teenagers are having.

(2) Complete the form on pages 137–138.

(3) Answer this question: "What happened in these observed settings that caused the children or teenagers to be so interested in, excited about, concerned about, committed to, involved in, and fascinated with what they were doing?" Also consider that if some of the young people observed were not fully interested or excited, why not? What could have been done to involve them?

(4) For each of the items listed in #3 as what was happening to cause the young people to be interested, excited, concerned, committed, involved, and fascinated, think of and write two ways that a teacher could implement that in a classroom.

(5) With all these ideas about how children and teenagers do get interested in and fascinated with part of their lives, plan a three-dimensional lesson using the forms on pages 76–82 and pages 140–141.

(6) This step is optional, but helpful. The teacher who is involved in the self-teaching watches a video of a lesson and critiques that lesson using the three-dimensional process. If this is not available, have the teacher observe colleagues who are already teaching so that their students are fascinated with learning.

(7) The teacher implements his or her three-dimensional lesson and has invited a very capable colleague to observe. After class he or she will evaluate the lesson. Some evaluation materials are below.

Evaluation of First Dimension

A Variety of Purposefully Planned Activities

(1) The idea that would be learned through this lesson was clearly identified
_____ yes _____ no
and was clearly communicated to students
_____ yes _____ no

(2) The activities that were used were
supportive of the purpose of the lesson _____ yes _____ no
varied (more than one; more than one type) _____ yes _____ no
clearly communicated to students so students understood the purpose of each activity _____ yes _____ no
and so students understood the procedures for each activity
_____ yes _____ no

(3) Student understanding of the purpose and the procedure of each activity was confirmed by the teacher _____ yes _____ no;
If yes, explain how. _____

(4) Interaction caused by this lesson included the following:

	Student	*Teacher*	*Idea*	*Activity*
Student	How did students interact with students?	How did the students interact with the teacher?	How did students interact with the idea?	How did students interact with and in the activity?
Teacher	How did the teacher interact with the students?	Applies only in team-teaching or collaboration?	How did the teacher interact with the idea?	How did the teacher interact with and in the activity?

(5) Learning was measured by what means? _____

_____

Learning was confirmed by what means? _____

_____

Evaluation of Second Dimension (relates to third)

The Activities Are Meaningful, Energetic, and Dramatic

(1) Warm-up: What did the students and the teacher do to warm-up their minds, attitudes, attention, and energy at the very start of the lesson?

_____

_____

_____

(2) Drills: What drill activity did the teacher and students use to work on specific information and/or abilities? _____

_____

_____

(3) Skills: What did the teacher and students to do apply information and abilities? _____

_____

_____

(4) Scrimmage: What did the teacher and the students do to demonstrate mastery of the purpose of the lesson? _____

_____

_____

(5) Cool-down: What did the teacher and the students do to extend their learning beyond the lesson and to synthesize/review all learning in this lesson? extend: _____

_____

synthesize/review: _____

_____

(6) Huddle: What did the teacher and the students do to accept responsibility for and build commitment to their work for tomorrow and beyond? _____

_____

_____

Evaluation of Third Dimension (relates to second):

Uses Interaction to Inform, Amaze, Exercise, Apply,
and Challenge the Mind of Each Student

(1) In what way and through what action did the teacher cause interaction that informed, amazed, exercised, applied, and challenged the mind of each student?

	Interaction
That informed the mind of each student	
That amazed the mind of each student	
That exercised the mind of each student	
That applied the mind of each student	
That challenged the mind of each student	

(2) What action was done by the teacher and the students that coincide with the thirty-two cells in the grid shown in Figure 6.1 on page 141.

MARKETING FASCINATION

How can students be prepared for experiences in fascinating classrooms at a fascinating school? Here's an idea from a consumer products company for which the author worked: sometimes, it helps consumers realize that a product is working if they are able to see some change occur as the product works. For example, when a cleaning product changes color, it suggests that something active is happening.

So, change the appearance of the school. Blank walls can be painted with pictures, words, or designs that intrigue students. What would be the impact of the word *think* or the word *learn* painted on walls in a school? What happens if the walls by the science rooms are covered with pictures that relate to science? Could the gym walls be covered with pictures of athletes?

Schools can appear to be rather bleak places. White walls, black lockers, and concrete block walls are not inspiring. Students could work with teachers to design and decorate classrooms and hallways. Businesses know that their appearance can create an atmosphere that is appealing to customers. Schools can do the same with very little money, but with a lot of creativity and involvement.

REWARDING FASCINATION

Also, schools usually get more of what they reward. When perfect attendance is rewarded, a larger number of students may work toward perfect attendance. So, reward fascination. Students who ask fascinating questions are entered in a drawing each week for a prize. Students who do fascinating work on an assignment get phone calls to their families with the good news (families rarely get good news phone calls from school despite lots of good that occurs daily at school). Teachers who present an especially fascinating lesson can be nominated by a student, a colleague, or an administrator for recognition. Each school can invent other ways to create a school atmosphere of fascination and to reward fascinating work based on the recognition methods that work best at that school.

CURRICULUM AND INSTRUCTION POLICIES

Some schools may decide to formally put into policies some actions that help implement three-dimensional teaching. For schools that use school-based decision making or other methods of decentralized management, policies about teaching could be enacted. Examples include the following:

(1) No more than 10% of class time may be spent on students reading the textbook in class.

(2) One worksheet per week is the maximum any teacher may use with any class.

(3) Each teacher will use at least ten different resources each week. Resources include, but are not limited to, (A) books, (B) computer programs, (C) discussions in class, (D) guest speakers, (E) textbooks, (F) newspapers and periodicals, (G) encyclopedias, (H) student writings, (I) dissertations and other research, (J) demonstrations, (K) competitive academic games, (L) lectures, (M) tests, and (N) films, video cassettes, audio cassettes, or other audio-visual materials.

(4) At least 30% of each student's overall grade in each class is based on writing assignments.

(5) All tests and quizzes must be teacher made and cannot be publisher made.

(6) All homework, tests, quizzes, and other work is graded and is returned to students within 2 days of when it was handed in.

This chapter has emphasized the process of professional development training that can help a faculty, a smaller group of teachers, or just one teacher implement three-dimensional teaching. This chapter presented evaluation tools that can help monitor the implementation of three-dimensional teaching. This chapter also considered ways to communicate to students that school is fascinating and that learning at school is fascinating.

The next chapter concludes this adventure with some very specific challenges to and duties for students. The chapter ends with a story that will have a different ending for each reader.

CHAPTER 7

The Fascinating Adventure

For many students, school is boring. For many teachers, students seem to be apathetic, disconnected, bored. Students would prefer that school provided fascinating experiences that capture their interest and that gain their commitment. Students do have interests and do make commitments. If school were fascinating, school could interest students and could receive a commitment from students.

Most teachers would prefer that students show some intellectual grasp of and interest in the curriculum, the work in classes, and the assignments for classes. Sure, some teachers have arranged an unspoken bargain with students—I will not expect much work from you, I will not do much work for you, you will pass the class, I will get paid, just don't cause any problems. The author hopes that most teachers still seek ways to improve their own work.

This book provides a method of teaching and a mentality about teaching that says that what students seek—a school that is not boring—and what teachers seek—students who are not bored—can both be caused through teaching that fascinates. The research included in this book, the Interaction Lesson Plan—Basic Concept and Instruction Grid, the six-part sequence, the student conversations with Jared and his friends, the faculty lounge discussions, the lesson plan practicing, and the professional development process are all designed to remind teachers that our original bold dream on the first day of our teaching career—to cause learning in the life of each student—is valid, is possible, and is the standard our work must uphold.

Chapter 7 is a collection of calls to action and benedictions (A) for teachers who will renew or who will begin for the first time a commitment to make school fascinating, to make their teaching fascinating, to fascinate their students, and to always be the great teacher they originally promised themselves they would be and (B) for students whose lives would be greatly enhanced by making and keeping a commitment to this idea about school—results, not excuses.

FOR too many students, school is the enemy. That must change. Educators can cite endless reasons that explain why teaching is more demanding than it ever was. Educators can claim that all students should come to school ready and eager to learn. Educators can criticize lazy, defiant, spoiled, out of control, impolite, delinquent students and the equally disorderly parents/guardians of those students. Educators can say that the present conditions are bad and that the future looks dark.

We can curse the darkness, or we can light a candle. The author suggests that we light many fascinating candles that illuminate the fascinating adventure of learning.

Schools need more drama, excitement, intensity, and energy. School is boring. Learning is fascinating. Sure, schools cannot match the special effects thrills of the latest Hollywood blockbuster action movie, but schools can do a lot better than worksheets and textbooks, day after day, week after week.

Schools have a resource, a tool, a method that Hollywood does not have, that television does not have, that computers do not have, and that compact discs do not have.

Schools have endless opportunities for direct, meaningful, purposeful, dramatic, energetic, intense human-to-human interaction. It is through this compelling interaction of student and teacher as they pursue the fascinating adventure of ideas, thoughts, knowing, exploring, wondering, learning, failing, and succeeding that schools can become absolutely fascinating and that learning at school can become a fascinating experience that students value and commit to.

Students are real people living real lives. They have ideas and feelings, hopes and hurts, brains and souls, pasts and futures. Students may not realize it yet, but teachers are on their side. Students and teachers can team-up in the fascinating adventure of causing learning.

Coaches ask athletes to give 110% and to be leaders. The same can be expected of students. Teachers can use the material below with students to start the process of creating championship students by making students aware of what they can be. The material below about 110% leadership may also remind teachers of what they can be.

———————————

110% LEADERSHIP

110%—to do better, to do more, to excel. To constantly ask yourself, "Am I doing the best I can do? Am I being the best I can be? Am I doing more than is required?"

110% is not about being better than someone else. There will always be someone who scores higher or lower than you do. 110% is about doing better today than you did yesterday. 110% is about demanding that you not accept a D grade when you can make a C or a B grade when you can make an A.

110% means that you come to school, even if you would prefer to sleep late. 110% means that you get to school on time and that you get to each class on time. 110% means that you take school seriously—sure, there will be some laughs and some good times, but school is about learning and learning requires work.

110% is uncommon. Many people settle for getting by, for good enough, or for what is easy. 110% takes you to a level of greatness. 110% challenges you and then enables you to become what you were always capable of becoming.

Leadership: doing what is right, in the right way, for benefit to myself and to other people.

To be a leader is to do what is right.

To be a leader is to do what is right, in the right way.

To be a leader is to do what is right, in the right way, for benefit to myself and to other people.

It is my duty to lead a good life right now, a productive life now, a purposeful life now, a life that shows progress now, and a life that shows results now. In order to lead this good life now, I must do what is right. This means that I obey rules, that I get my work done completely, that I turn in my work on time, that I do not harm any other person in any way including what I say or what I do, and that I respect other people.

Respecting a teacher means that I do not disrupt class. Respecting a teacher means that I come to class prepared—I bring paper, pencil, pen, and book. I leave social conversations for a later time, such as lunch or after school. I listen in class. I participate in class properly. I work in class. I ask sensible, important questions. I think. I learn.

Respecting a teacher means that I do not talk back, I do not show off, and I do not act silly. When the teacher says "start working," I start working instantly. I do not waste time, I do not talk, I do not bother people, and I do not spend a few minutes getting ready to start working. I stay ready. I stay ready always. I start working as soon as the teacher says, "start working."

Being a student who leads means following the teacher and following the rules.

How do I apply the ideas and the ideals of 110% leadership to my work at school and to my life in general? Each letter in the word *LEADERSHIP* stands for another word. Read on for the details.

L = Listen:

- in class to the teacher
- at home to parents(s), guardian(s)
- to myself when I am thinking honestly

How do I listen best in class? By paying total attention to the teacher. I look at the person who is talking to me. I take notes. I think about what people are saying to me. I ask a question. I answer a question. I ask myself, "What conclusion are we reaching?"

When I do not listen, it is because _____

_____

I would listen better if I would _____

_____

E = Education:

The purpose of a school is to cause learning.

School is not my personal place to show off, to act foolish, to embarrass my family, to get in trouble, to waste time, to hit people, to insult people, or to bother people. Nobody comes to school to see me perform, to see me get in trouble, or to have me steal from them or to have me intimidate them.

I am not the star of the show at school. If I do my work well, if I obey the rules of school, if I cooperate with people, I can become a superstar at school and move on to greater success.

At school, I can do what is right, in the right way, for myself and for other people. I can lead, and I can learn. I can give 110% of myself to succeeding at school, and I can get an education that will benefit me and other people for a lifetime.

A = Attitude:

The 110% leadership attitude is

- positive
- cooperative
- determined
- energetic
- persistent
- confident
- optimistic

My attitude will never be, "Well, other people are goofing off, why can't I? Other people steal, why can't I? Other people cheat, smoke, lie, or skip school, why can't I?"

I am not other people. Their mistakes do not give me permission to make mistakes.

I am me. I am not other people. I am going to be the best me I can be. I know what is right, and I will do what is right.

My attitude is, "I will do what is right, in the right way, for myself, and for other people."

D = Discipline:

The school has rules, and I will obey the rules.

The school district has rules, and I will obey those also.

The city and the state have laws. I will obey those laws.

I will do more than the rules and the laws require of me.

I will obey every rule, but I will follow a greater rule.

I will obey every law, but I will follow a greater law.

I will do what is right, in the right way, at all times, for myself and for other people.

I will give 110% effort, always.

My rule is to always do what is right, in the right way, for myself, and for other people. My law is to give 110%, always.

E = Example:

I like for people to be friendly to me, so I will be friendly to other people. I will not pretend to be friendly, I will be genuine.

I like for people to listen to me, to respect me, to encourage me. I will listen to, respect, and encourage other people.

I get tired of students who fight, steal, curse, insult, disrupt class, threaten people, disrespect the teachers, intimidate you to get money, try to sell you drugs, or lie about you. I will not do any of that.

I will lead by example. If other people do what is wrong, I will still do what is right. I may have to work harder now than people who cheat. I may have to do without things now that people who steal have. I am not a cheater, and I am not a thief.

I am me, and this me does what is right. I lead by example because I am leading me, and I deserve the best. I am going to follow me so I have to lead me correctly. You may also follow me so I owe you the best example I can set.

R = Responsibility:

The 110% leadership definition of the word *responsibility* is, "results, not excuses."

That is all. I will make no excuses. I will not let other people make excuses for me. I will get results, the right results, in the right way.

When my homework is due in 3 days, I will begin today, and I will have that homework completed before it is due. When my class starts in 3 minutes, I will arrive in 1 minute and use the extra time for extra preparation. My job, my challenge, is to get results.

I am better than any excuse. It is too easy to say, "Nobody told me about the paper that is due. Nobody told me to attend the meeting. Nobody reminded me to return the book. Nobody told me what the rule is."

I do not expect people to tell me or remind me. I know what I am responsible for, I write it down, I monitor my progress, and I am ahead of every deadline. I know what the rules are, but I behave better than the rules require.

I get results, I do not make excuses.

S = Study:

There are three sources of intelligence, according to Dr. David Perkins, in his fine book *Outsmarting IQ:* (1) the mental ability/potential you are born with, (2) the experiences, including school, you have in your life, and (3) the amount of and the quality of thinking and reflection you do.

I am in total control of how much work I do for school and of how much serious, productive thinking I do. There is no limit to how much I can learn if I set no limits on how much I study, think, write, work, and use my brain. I can know as much as any human has ever known, if I will study enough.

I will read while others watch endless television. I will write while others listen to endless music. Sure, I'll watch some television, and I will listen to some music, but only for entertainment or for a reward, not as a lifestyle.

I challenge myself to learn more than I ever thought I could learn. Sure, it will be lots of work, but I am worth it. When I study, it makes me smarter, wiser, better. I am worth that effort because I deserve to be smarter, wiser, better.

It is right to study. I will do what is right. I will study. I will study in the right way—read and read again because no person fully understands what is read the first time. I will take notes. I will complete all assignments. I will write rough drafts. I will ask the teacher to explain to me anything that I do incorrectly, and then I will turn in the corrections to be sure that I am right.

I will study, then I will study more, and only then will I have earned a rest and a break.

H = Homework:

I will do my homework.

I will do all of my homework.

I will do all of my homework, on time.

I will turn in all of my homework, on time.

I will write down each assignment before I leave each class. I will check my assignment list before I leave school so I have all books and supplies I will need.

I will begin my homework soon after I arrive at home. I will not wait until after supper or after watching hours of television before I start my homework. I will create a schedule for the hours of the afternoon and the evening so I know what work will be done at what time and so I can also plan some time off.

If I have time at school during a class, while I wait for a ride home, or while I wait for an activity to start, I will begin my homework. I will use my time now for work so I will have time later for hobbies, games, or just doing nothing.

I will do my homework, and I will be proud of my results.

I = Instructions:

This is simple—teachers give me instructions for reasons. I will follow their instructions.

The school gives me instructions for reasons. I will follow the school's instructions.

I would lose much time and I could cause problems if I constantly question why I have to follow instructions. I can probably figure out why an instruction is given, but my responsibility is to do what I am instructed to do. I will do that. I will follow instructions, and I will get results, even if other people decide to not follow the instructions.

I know this truth—when I follow the instructions from my teacher, from the principal, or from other people in authority at school, life is simpler, we all get along better, and I stay out of trouble.

P = Polite:

Please and thank you still work and still are right. I will say "please," and I will say "thank you."

When I am wrong, I will say "I'm sorry. I was wrong." I will also ask, "How can I make up for what I did?" and I will do what is needed to correct my mistake.

Even if I think it was not completely my fault or even if I got caught while other people did not get caught, I will do what is right, simple and peaceful. I will say, "I'm sorry. I was wrong. How can I make up for what happened?" By doing that, I will help solve the problem. That will be simpler, that will be more peaceful and then we can all move past the problem.

Being polite at school is right, and I must do what is right. I will lead by example, and that includes being polite to people.

It is right to hold a door for someone else. It is right to help a person pick up what he or she dropped. It is right to wait to be called on in class before I speak. It is right to be polite.

I can avoid making a mess in the cafeteria, but if I do make a mess I can clean it up. I don't use curse words. I don't tell dirty jokes. I don't bother people, steal from people, or play silly jokes on people. I don't make ugly or insulting comments about people.

If people are impolite to me, I can still be polite to them.

I ask people if they would please do something for me. I don't command them or tell them or yell at them or argue with them.

Being polite really is easy—I treat people with the decency and with the respect that I hope people will treat me with.

I am a leader. I do what is right. I am polite. This includes how I treat other students. This certainly includes how I treat adults, including my family. If I make a phone call to my family, I will be polite. I do not say, "Come get me." I say, "I'm sorry if it is inconvenient, but I need a ride home. Could you pick me up at school, please? Thank you."

I have been taught right from wrong. I will do what is right, in the right way, for the benefit of myself and of other people.

Students may still ask, "Well, in football, we are shown exactly how to block and exactly how to tackle. Teachers never do that. They say write a report or do these problems. Why can't teachers tell us like coaches do?"

OK. The list below is for teachers to share with students who ask the question, "What am I supposed to do?" or who need to be told what to do.

Conscientious, caring, wonderful teachers and those teachers who are less than conscientious, caring, and wonderful could easily join in a loud complaint: "Wait a minute. The school already gives each student a chance to learn and to succeed. If we make changes and do the work that helps fascinate students, but some students still do nothing, what will change for them. Sure, they *can* learn, but they won't work enough to learn. The student and the parent(s) or guardian(s) must take a lot of responsibility."

That is true. Schools do present opportunities for each student to learn; however, schools pay teachers to cause learning so there is a contractual, professional, and employment reality, which suggests that teachers must relentlessly seek ways to cause learning in the mind of each student.

Every student can learn. Every student who is taught by a teacher who fascinates, who inspires, who amazes, who plans thoroughly, who captivates, who convinces students that learning at school is worthwhile and is worth the effort will learn. At least, they will learn more than they would in a boring classroom.

Every student can learn. Every student who will get to class on time, arrive in class prepared, complete all homework, pay attention in class, read all assigned material, and stay out of trouble will learn. If they do all of that and they are fascinated by three-dimensional teaching, there is no limit to the learning.

This book has emphasized methods that teachers can use to fulfill the ideas that all students can learn and that all classrooms in all schools can be places where learning is caused. It is proper to directly address the reality that some students are not doing their share of the work. The following list is long, but still does not cover all the responsibilities that students must accept and all of the tasks that they must do; however, this list is a good start. Students, get to work—here's how:

(1) Sharpen your pencil before class.

(2) Don't wait until the night before a paper is due to begin the research.

(3) Sit in the front of the class if a seat is available, but from any seat do this: pay total attention to the teacher and to the work of that class.

(4) Being on time is good. Being early is great.

(5) Ignore students who try to distract you.

(6) Take notes. Review your notes.

(7) Ask questions that relate to the class.

(8) Participate in class discussions that are led by the teacher.

(9) Do not pass social notes to other students. Passing notes means failing scores on tests or getting in other trouble.

(10) Don't ask if you can go to the bathroom. You can wait. Teachers have better uses of their abilities than deciding whether you really have to go.

(11) When the principal asks, "Did you do that?" say, "Yes, sir," or "Yes, ma'am," if you did that. Say "No, sir," or "No, ma'am," if you are innocent.

(12) Do not loan money to other students. It causes problems.

(13) Pay more attention.

(14) When a teacher assigns material for you to read as homework, read it, twice.

(15) Ask your teachers to give you more work to do. More work!

(16) Don't slam your locker. That causes noise pollution.

(17) Wear clothes that encourage you to be in the mood to learn. Avoid clothes that feel like summer vacation.

(18) Do not wear clothes with any disruptive brand logo, music group, cartoon, or saying printed on it.

(19) Get to know the school's main office secretary. She can do favors for you.

(20) Stay off the phone at home until your homework is finished.

(21) Study in study hall.

(22) If you have a part-time job, be sure it does not prevent you from being a full-time student.

(23) You are right—school is not always "fair" in your opinion. So what? Are you always fair? Be honest, didn't you make your little brother

take the blame when you broke your mother's lamp under threat that you would beat him up?

(24) Sensible and proper dating is great, but be cool; keep your hands off each other most of the time during school so your minds can be on school.

(25) If you don't like the cafeteria food, quit complaining, and make your own lunch each morning to bring with you.

(26) Some of the comments that pop into your brain should not pop out of your mouth.

(27) Don't give excuses. Just say, "I don't have the assignment done. May I turn it in tomorrow, please, for a grade no higher than B?"

(28) Teachers are smarter than you are, so far. Until you catch up—which they are trying to enable you to do—be humble.

(29) Be polite.

(30) Be very friendly to those students of whom everyone makes fun and who nobody likes. Those people will love you forever. At the 15th class reunion, you'll be the only person who does not have to apologize.

(31) If you think a teacher is boring, you might be correct, but guess what he or she thinks of you? The teacher could be showing more life than you are.

(32) Sports are played. Life is not. Get serious.

(33) Taking drugs is dumb. If you take drugs, you are acting dumb, and then you are dead.

(34) Alcohol is a drug. It can kill you.

(35) Sex before marriage causes problems. Sex outside of marriage causes problems. Safe sex isn't safe. Just don't.

(36) Do more than is assigned, required, and expected.

(37) Join a club that does something good for other people.

(38) Skip cigarettes, don't skip classes.

(39) Think.

(40) It is legal in the United States to leave your TV set turned off for a complete day.

(41) AIDS and other epidemics of sexually transmitted diseases came after rock 'n roll, pornography, trash television/movies, and the new morality. Don't you wonder?

(42) Study. Study more. Keep studying.

(43) Sure, he said, "I love you." That is not what he meant.

(44) If you would not take your basketball shoes off and leave the court before the final buzzer, why would you put up your books and start getting ready to leave class before the bell rings?

(45) You like some teachers more than you like others. Guess what? Teachers like some students more than they like others. The difference is they teach every student. You may not work for and cooperate with the teachers you don't like. Change that.

(46) The purpose is to get an education. The purpose is not to like everyone or to be amused or to have fun. Those may happen, but make education happen first.

(47) Don't wear clothes that reveal what is or is not there.

(48) School is not fun. Doing well in school is. First, do well in school, then you'll realize the joy.

(49) Homework is work to be done at home. It is work. That's why we call it homework.

(50) Listen to the announcements.

(51) Arrive before school starts, and stay until it is over.

(52) Leaving campus for lunch is not worth it and is often not allowed. Save the dollars, the gasoline, and the time.

(53) If you try out for anything and do not make it, volunteer to help. You will still be involved and if a big opportunity occurs, you'll be there.

(54) Don't say anything about anyone. It *always* causes problems.

(55) When you take a foreign language class, above all else, learn the vocabulary. If you know the words, the rest will come.

(56) When math and science do not make sense, have a student who understands them teach you. These subjects are just different from every other topic. Sometimes, only a student can explain these subjects to a student who is having trouble.

(57) Cover your mouth when you cough in class. Cover your nose when you sneeze in class.

(58) If you think you are about to vomit, you do not have to ask permission to leave class. Run out of the classroom pointing to your puffy cheeks, but do not fake it.

(59) Do not make bodily noises in a classroom, especially those associated with odor. Noises and the odors cannot hide, neither can you.

(60) Dating is part of being a teenager, but don't spend all of your money or all of your time on your social life.

(61) Study before each test. Preferably, study several days before a test, and spend the rest of the time reviewing.

(62) You heard that your teacher never gives a pop quiz. Wrong.

(63) Spelling counts.

(64) "Whatdidyagit" is not the proper comment when tests are being returned. Silence is proper.

(65) Cheating is cheating. Quit.

(66) Did you hear about the student who cheated all through school, graduated from Harvard, and was a millionaire by age 30? Do you know why you never heard of this student?

(67) Do not say ain't.

(68) Clean up your language.

(69) Eat healthy food. Candy and pop, chips and cookies are not the four food groups. They are OK, but eat some real food, too.

(70) If you come to school for any reason other than to learn, you should still come, but keep your mouth shut, don't steal anything, and leave people alone. Be on time so the rest of us are not bothered by your irresponsibility.

(71) Type papers whether they have to be typed or not. Typing is impressive.

(72) Wear clothes that match.

(73) Wear clothes that do not bring attention to you.

(74) The teacher is the manager of his or her classroom. You are visiting his or her home. Be a courteous and appreciative guest.

(75) Write down the homework assignments before you leave each class. Check that list, and get all books you need before you leave school.

(76) Keep all papers and tests that teachers return to you. Keep a record of each grade you get in each class. This avoids the question that teachers hate, "What's my grade in your class?"

(77) Items that are not taken to school by serious students: gum, candy, cigarettes, alcohol, other drugs, pornography, records, cassettes, compact discs, radios, electronic equipment, televisions, paging devices, portable phones, guns, knives, other weapons.

(78) Items which are taken to school by serious students: notebook, textbook, paper, pencils, pens, manners, responsibility, work ethic, energy.

(79) Until you have read every book in the school library, it is a lie to say, "There's nothing to do."

(80) When you are studying, write information on 3 × 5 index cards. Carry these cards in your pocket. When you are waiting for anything, take the cards out and read them.

(81) Do not begin your comment with, "This may be a dumb question, but. . . ." The question is fine, unless you convince us otherwise.

(82) Say "thank you" when teachers hand out material in class.

(83) When teachers write comments on your papers they graded, read the comments, and talk to the teachers about them.

(84) Write down everything that teachers write on the chalkboard.

(85) Being old enough to drive does not necessarily mean being smart and responsible enough to drive.

(86) Limit your school evening activities. The best place to be on any evening before a school day is at home.

(87) Joining a mob of 18,000 screaming, smoking, cursing, grabbing, under-the-influence concert goers for a loud, crude, vulgar, expensive tribal ritual can cause problems. Pick concerts that are fun, not frenzied.

(88) One month ago, the teacher assigned a report. It is due tomorrow. You are not finished, so you plan to "play sick" tomorrow. Grow up. Finish the work. Go to school. Get real. Start early next time.

(89) There is plenty of time for people who plan, prepare, and say no.

(90) Lock your locker.

(91) "Is the test easy?" If you are prepared for the test, yes, it will be easy. If you are not prepared for the test, it will be difficult.

(92) Study on weekends and during vacations. Get ahead.

(93) During the summer, read the books you asked your teachers to recommend. Be sure to ask for their recommendations each May.

(94) Select one bad habit that prevents you from being a great student, such as gazing out a window during classes, and just quit it, now!

(95) Take books home even when you have no homework and read ahead.

(96) The answer to, "What did you do in school today?" begins with these two words: "A lot . . ." and continues with complete details.

(97) When you are accused of breaking a rule or of other misbehavior, tell the truth, the whole truth, and nothing but the truth. Do not argue. Do not confront.

(98) "Do unto others as you would have them do unto you." Get it? Treat people the way you hope to be treated.

(99) Adults think, act, talk, and live differently from you. The adults are not going to move back to younger years. You are moving toward adult years. The truth is you have to move up to their level, so start now, today, in at least one way.

(100) Talk to the best students in your school. Find out what they do to be successful in school. Imitate their methods that are honest, ethical, and effective.

(101) "Just say know" as in "I know I can do this" and "I'm going to know everything about each subject I study," or "I don't know yet, but I'll read a book tonight and find out."

(102) Substitute good habits for bad habits.

(103) Have an apple instead of a second serving of french fries.

(104) Take a nap instead of watching another show on TV.

(105) Read a book instead of watching another hour of music videos.

(106) Wash the dishes after supper instead of running out of the house with an, "I gotta go."

(107) Stay home with your family instead of going to every school sporting event.

(108) Read.

(109) Quote brilliant thinkers and accomplished doers instead of talk show hosts, actors, or musicians.

(110) Read a newspaper instead of goofing off.

(111) Complete a commitment instead of quitting.

(112) Save money instead of spending it.

(113) Exercise for an hour, then hang out with friends. Hanging out is not exercise.

(114) Take vitamins instead of drugs.

(115) Do what you are told the first time you are told instead of the fifth time.

(116) Say nothing instead of curse words.

(117) Say " yes" instead of "yeah."

(118) Now, say, "yes, sir" instead of "yes."

(119) Ask "May I talk with you?" instead of interrupting.

(120) Write a letter instead of making a long-distance call, just to see what it is like.

(121) Send a greeting card you made instead of one you purchased.

(122) Give a gift you made instead of one you bought.

(123) Walk out of a movie that is awful, and request a refund from the manager.

(124) Work on a farm 1 week in the summer.

(125) Get down on the floor and play a game with your little brother, sister, or neighbor. Teach them something important and let them teach you.

(126) End each day with thanks.

(127) Begin each day with hope.

(128) Continue each day with persistence.

(129) Before leaving school, occasionally ask teachers or other staff members if there is any task you could do for them.

(130) Participation in sports and in clubs can be very beneficial, but please remember that your diploma is based on your report card, not your free throws or your class presidency. Get involved in school, but do not try to do everything.

(131) If you get a low grade on a test or other assignment, avoid blaming the teacher, the other students, the school, the textbook, the class schedule, the sport you play, or the club of which you are a member. Accept the responsibility for learning what the test shows you do not yet know. Be better prepared for the next test. Remember, "Results, not excuses."

(132) "What grade did you give me?" Wrong question. Teachers do not give grades. Teachers calculate the grade you earned.

(133) It is tougher to be a teenager now than ever before. It's also tougher to be an adult. The obvious idea is to team-up with your parent(s) or guardian(s) and with teachers. If you fight them, you lose. If you team-up with them, everyone wins.

(134) If you still have the television on, turn it off for 1 hour.

(135) If you still have music playing, turn that off for 1 hour.

(136) If you are still on the phone, hang up for 1 hour.

(137) Now, treat yourself to an evening of no noise, no places to go, some books to read, much silence, and begin exercising your mind.

(138) On the day after your first evening of silent reading and thinking, have another evening of silent reading and thinking. You may re-read some material and experience that deep learning that scholars seek.

(139) Enough advice. Get to work.

Students: Please note the 139 ideas can be implemented with no new laws and no new taxes. The 139 ideas await your commitment and effort. The ultimate reformer of your education is you.

The fascinating adventure that school can become includes teachers who see their duty as causing learning. These teachers know that if learning is not caused, they did not teach. They may have been busy and active, they may have done lots of work with, to, or for students, but the bottom line for a conscientious teacher is, "Did I cause each student to learn?"

The fascinating adventure also includes students who accept their responsibilities. Part of a teacher's job in causing learning is to so effectively interact with students that they do accept their responsibilities.

The fascinating adventure ideally includes supportive and involved parents, guardians, school boards, school district administrators, communities, political leaders, professional groups, college and university schools of education, and others in higher education. This book emphasized teaching, so this book concentrated on teachers and students.

This chapter concludes with a story, but each reader will create his or her unique conclusion to the story and therefore to the book. This is a realistic reminder that your classroom, your students, your teaching, your school will be as fascinating as you decide to make it and will have as much learning as you commit yourself to cause.

Kelly

It was Friday afternoon about 3:30, and my classroom was quiet. It had been a long day and a very long week. I was exhausted and ready to go home. A few more chores to finish, and the day would be over.

I did not expect anyone to come in my room, so the knock on the door surprised me. Maybe someone was having car trouble, or maybe another teacher just wanted to visit.

"Well, hi, Kelly. What brings you here on Friday after school?"

"I dunno. Just hanging out."

"Do you have any weekend plans, Kelly?"

"Maybe." Kelly paused, and the silence suggested there was more Kelly was thinking.

"What's on your mind, Kelly?" I asked, but I was not really prepared for the answer.

"I hate school. I really hate it. People are mean. There are too many rules. I get in trouble a lot. I make bad grades. And everything is so dull. This place is dead. It's boring here."

I look at Kelly and realized that this student was telling the truth, the whole truth, and nothing but the truth for Kelly. I love school, but Kelly genuinely hates it. I think school is a great place. It is awful for Kelly.

I knew what to say, and I also knew that this type of opportunity to encourage Kelly would never occur again. Kelly had spoken to me straight from the heart, so I spoke to Kelly with equal honesty.

"Kelly, . . .

SYSTEMIC reform of education can be necessary. This author would hope that the goal of such reform is to restructure the system to help cause learning by each student in each classroom in each school. Broad reform should pass the school purpose test—does it help cause learning?

The Kentucky Education Reform Act (KERA), passed in 1990, completely changed public schools in Kentucky. Although the reform has had some critics, the author's experience is that if a school completely and correctly implements KERA, the results are very favorable. Similar reforms have begun or are being considered in many other states, school districts, or schools.

The type of teaching that KERA and some comparable reforms expect is very similar to the type of teaching created by the three-dimensional model in this book. The following perspective is provided to show that educational reform that concentrates on what teachers and students do in the classroom can be very successful.

KERA AND BERA—A STORY OF REFORM

No state in the nation is implementing an education reform that is as comprehensive as Kentucky's education reform—the Kentucky Education Reform Act—which became law in July 1990. Polling information from 1995 indicates that only 50% of Kentuckians are aware of Kentucky's education reform. Other states are also developing or implementing substantial statewide educational reform. Public awareness of, understanding of, involvement in, and confidence in education reform are important elements of successful reform.

People often oppose what they do not understand. People can support what they understand or, if they are not supportive, they could offer helpful suggestions for improvement. Toward the goals of improved awareness and improved understanding of KERA in particular and of educational reform in general, the following story of reform is provided.

Basketball Excellence Results Activities (BERA)

"The problem is not free throws. I know that our players can hit free throws, at least they can hit them in practice. I've watched almost all of our players hit nine out of ten free throws in drills and in practice. So why do they hit 57% of their free throws in games? Why can't they apply in a game what they work on in practice?"

Good question, coach. Standing at the free throw line at practice and hitting 90% of the shots is a start, but if you cannot apply that skill in a game, more work is needed.

"Plus, we don't make good team decisions in games. We don't see the open player. We take bad shots. We have to call a time out and tell the players that the other team just changed their offense or their defense. Why can't our players think for themselves out on the basketball court?"

Another good question, coach. Your players need to be able to think, to solve problems that come up in a game, and to communicate with each other. You can help them learn a lot about basketball, but you also have to prepare them to think, to deal with new circumstances, and to work together.

"This game has changed so much over the years. When I played and then when I started coaching, basketball was a simple game of dribbling, passing, two-point shots, free throws, rebounds, and playing defense. Now, the game is more complex than ever with dozens of defenses, two types of guards, two types of forwards, three-point shots, and every player trying to imitate what he or she sees on television. How do I prepare players for all of today's new, complex situations and for others that will be invented in the future?"

Coach, complex challenges cannot be fully met with simple solutions. New challenges cannot be fully met with just more of the same old solutions. Some of the tried and true methods can still help, but your players will need new methods and new types of training also.

"I also coach the softball team. Those players need new uniforms and lots of new equipment. There are thirty-two softball players on the varsity and junior varsity teams, and the budget is $800. In basketball, our boys' teams have twenty-four players, and their budget is $3,250. The girls basketball teams have twenty-two players, and their budget is $2,800. Basketball teams need their money, but how can softball get better with such a small budget?"

Good point, coach. Extra money may not guarantee a winning record, but unless a team has enough money for the necessities, how can that team become the best it can be?

"OK, so what am I supposed to do? The basketball season is 1 month old. I have to concentrate on hoops now. I know that my team can do better than it is doing now. I know that we can win more games, and I'm sure that the players can work more as a team. What should I do?

Here are some suggestions. The purpose of these ideas is for the team to get excellent results (1) in their skills, (2) in their ability to work with each other as a team, (3) in their application of skills in games, and (4) in their overall results as a team—this includes improvement in practices and how well they perform in games. Remember, the intention is to get excellent results through these activities.

(1) Include drills at practice, but do more than drills only. Give the players more opportunities to apply the skills. Create more game situations for them to work through: we're behind by three points, 47 seconds left in the game, the other team in shooting a free throw; OK, team, what do you do?

(2) You want them to think on the court, so have them practice thinking. Do you ever give your team a written test? Try it. Give them ten game situations, and have them write their answer to what should be done. Go out on the court, and show them what their solutions would look like. They can learn from each other as each player presents an answer and as others evaluate it. After that, they decide which answer was best. Notice, coach, now they have learned about thinking, communicating, and working together.

(3) Set goals for the team, and have specific actions that need to be taken for each goal. For example, goal one: each student will keep grades high enough to remain eligible to play. Actions: the team has a study hall each day for 1 hour after school; the team begins study hall by making sure that each player knows what all assignments for tomorrow are; the team captain checks the attendance of each student and tells the coach if any player ever misses any class; the coach is given a copy of each test taken by each player after the test is graded and returned.

(4) Practices will have tests each week. Part of the test will be written; part of the test will be skills such as shooting free throws or shooting three-point shots; part of the test will be scrimmages; part of the test will be the team dealing with game situations that are simulated on the basketball court. The tests will measure how well our team is doing, not how each player is doing individually because basketball games are played by teams.

(5) Once per month during the season, the coach will meet with a group that includes all parents or guardians of the players and one teacher of each player. This coach/parent/teacher council will deal with any team concern, problem, or opportunity—not with concerns, problems, or opportunities about individual players; those will be dealt with separately—and will seek ideas for actions that can help the team.

(6) Once per week, the coach and the team will meet for an open discussion so any problems, tension, concerns, or misunderstandings can be dealt with. As needed, the coach may meet with groups of players or with individuals.

(7) The coach will work with the computer teacher to purchase some basketball videos and software programs that are not just games for entertainment, but are simulations of basketball games. The players will use these to think through how to deal with certain circumstances in a game.

(8) Extra Special Saturday—The players are told on Friday if they need to attend Extra Special Saturday, which is personalized instruction on Saturday morning from 8:00 to 10:00. This is not a punishment, and attendance must be agreed to by the player's family. This time helps players who need more individualized instruction than can usually be provided during Monday through Friday practices. A snack is served after these 2 hours of more individualized work. Some extra coaches, teachers, parents, or guardians will be there so players get more individualized coaching.

(9) The coach will attend more coaching clinics to learn more about basketball and about coaching.

(10) Rewards and intervention. Each week during the season, the coach and the team will set goals for the week. If the goals are reached, the team is rewarded. If the goals are not reached, there will be tougher practices the next week, and other work or other duties will be added. If we miss our goals 2 weeks in a row, the school's Athletic Director will attend practices and games to do some of the coaching. If that does not work, the Athletic Director will have full authority over the team until goals for a week are reached.

(11) To help finance all teams fairly, the school can establish one amount of money that each team will get per player on a team. Teams could raise more money than that amount, but at least each team would be given enough money to get the necessities for each player.

Basketball Excellence Results Activities (BERA) *and the Kentucky Education Reform Act (KERA)*

The eleven ideas that are presented above as BERA are modeled after eleven key parts of the Kentucky Education Reform Act. Certainly, a coach may find other methods for improving a team. The point of this essay is not to provide perfect athletic ideas, although some of the suggestions are worth considering by coaches.

Please remember, Kentucky is attempting to go beyond having students merely acquire information; rather, Kentucky seeks to enable students to understand, to think, to solve problems, to communicate, to apply knowledge, and to work well together. That sounds like three-dimensional teaching!

The purpose of this BERA essay is to help explain some of the key parts of KERA and to use an analogy with sports to show that reasoning behind those parts of KERA making school fascinating will largely depend on what happens in classrooms; however, classroom teaching changes are sometimes implemented as part of total systemic change. Also, systemic, organizational-structure change without classroom instruction change has a questionable likelihood of directly impacting the attitude of, commitment of, and learning by students. The items in numbers 1 through 11 in BERA match-up with the following parts of KERA. Look for similarities with three-dimensional teaching philosophy as practice while reading the following list.

(1) Performance events: students work together to solve a problem that requires communication, critical thinking, and cooperation.

(2) Open-ended questions: this type of question requires that a student, think, reason, give explanations, and consider alternatives. One important value of this questioning method is that students must apply information and show that they have an understanding, not just a recollection, of information.

(3) KERA has six goals that guide all instruction. The goals also have specific sub-goals called academic expectations.

(4) The Kentucky Instructional Results Information System (KIRIS) tests are given annually in Kentucky's public schools to assess how each school is doing. These tests assess performance, not recall, and these tests emphasize information about

the total school, not precise information about each student. The exact tests that have been used in Kentucky are being evaluated, and some content and/or format changes are likely, but this type of testing will continue probably.

(5) School-based decision making (SBDM) is Kentucky's version of decentralized management. By July 1996, 1,200 public schools in Kentucky had a school council of the principal, two parents, and three teachers making vital policy decisions in significant areas including curriculum and discipline.

(6) Family resource centers in elementary schools and youth service centers in secondary schools help provide and coordinate services to students and to families. These centers help schools work with the many situations that families and young people face in today's society, such as peer pressure, divorce, suicide, resolving conflicts, drug abuse, and job preparation.

(7) Kentucky's schools are implementing technology programs that include classroom use of computers, more computer labs, and interactive or networked teaching via computers.

(8) Extended school services is the part of Kentucky's reform that enables each school to design the plan that is best for its students who need additional time and assistance to succeed in school. This could mean a program that is conducted after school, on Saturday, or in the summer. The students work in small groups with one teacher and an average of eight students.

(9) Teachers, administrators, and other school personnel have attended many days of professional development training to learn how to implement the new teaching methods and the new management methods of KERA. Days have been included in the school calendar for this training.

(10) Part of the Kentucky plan is that schools are rewarded when they surpass their school goals on the KIRIS tests, and they can be assigned various levels of intervention by the Kentucky Department of Education if they fall short of those goals.

(11) Kentucky's funding of education has been changed significantly to reduce the gap between per pupil expenditure in the richest school districts versus the poorest school districts. The state's financing mechanism still permits local school districts to spend additional money as a local option beyond the level guaranteed by the state.

KEEN J. BABBAGE has taught social studies in grades 7–12. He has also taught education classes at the college and graduate levels. He has school administration experience with grades 6–12. He has executive experience with three large corporations.

Dr. Babbage has earned degrees from Centre College, Xavier University, and the University of Kentucky. His doctoral work at Kentucky was during 1989–1993 as the Kentucky Education Reform Act was developed, approved, and initially implemented.

Dr. Babbage's dissertation dealt with the public policy process of implementing school-based decision making. Dr. Babbage has written two previous books, both published in 1996 by Technomic Publishing Company, Inc.: *911—The School Administrator's Guide to Crisis Management* and *Meetings for School-Based Decision Making.*

He lives and works in Lexington, Kentucky.